# A JOSHUA
## GENERATION:

"Be strong and very courageous. Be careful to
obey all the law my servant Moses gave you; do
not turn from it to the right or to the left, that you
may be successful wherever you go. Do not let this
Book of the Law depart from your mouth; meditate on it day and night, so that you may be careful to do everything written in it. Then you will
be prosperous and successful" (Joshua 1:7–8).

## A STUDY GUIDE

# MOLLY HARDIN

WESTBOW
PRESS®
A DIVISION OF THOMAS NELSON
& ZONDERVAN

Unless otherwise indicated, Bible quotations are taken from New International Version Study Bible. Copyright (c) 1985, 1995, 2002 by Zondervan.

Unless otherwise indicated, Greek or Hebrew translations were taken from Strong's Exhaustive Concordance of the Bible. Copyright by Hendrickson Publishers. Additional studies and some definitions were taken from Strong's Concordance as listed on www.blueletterbible.org.

Some principles are duplicated from the companion book titled A Joshua Generation. Copyright is provided by the same company and author.

Pictures for this cover were taken by Sam Gromko of samGfotografie.

WestBow Press books may be ordered through booksellers or by contacting:

WestBow Press
A Division of Thomas Nelson & Zondervan
1663 Liberty Drive
Bloomington, IN 47403
www.westbowpress.com
1 (866) 928-1240

Because of the dynamic nature of the Internet, any web addresses or links contained in this book may have changed since publication and may no longer be valid. The views expressed in this work are solely those of the author and do not necessarily reflect the views of the publisher, and the publisher hereby disclaims any responsibility for them.

Any people depicted in stock imagery provided by Thinkstock are models, and such images are being used for illustrative purposes only. Certain stock imagery © Thinkstock.

ISBN: 978-1-4908-9728-8 (sc)
ISBN: 978-1-4908-9729-5 (e)

Print information available on the last page.

WestBow Press rev. date: 09/16/2015

To "the pilot group."
You guys have been amazing.
I asked you to participate in hopes that I
could teach you something.
I didn't realize how much you would
be teaching me. I am so grateful that
God has given me the opportunity of having
a place in each of your lives.

# Acknowledgments

Sam Gromko of samGfotografie took pictures for this cover and website. You can view her amazing talent at www.samgfoto.com. Thanks for being a friend to me and this vision throughout the years.

Kyrios Media designed and managed our website www.myjoshuaproject.com. You guys are amazing. Thank you again for everything.

Thank you to my biggest fans: Marty, Mason, and Drew. Every day I am better because of you.

# Table of Contents

Week Eight

# Introduction

Many times I have sat in my living room full of teenagers and have listened to their stories of past failures and convictions. I have witnessed and counseled them with encouraging words that God gives grace and tomorrow He'll give another chance for them to act according to His word. Oftentimes, these second chances end in condemnation and regrets.

As I prayed for their strength night after night, I asked myself the questions, "What if they don't know how to make the right choices? What if they don't have the right tools for success? Do they know how to lead?" Through those nights, God laid on my heart a curriculum to provide these young adults with the necessary equipment for days of victories. From that program of study, this workbook was born. This workbook was written for those of you who want to be the leader God created you to be, but struggle with consistently making the best decision.

I do not have all the answers, and all circumstances are different, but God gives a list of simple step-by-step instructions on how to defeat Satan and temptations in your life. By creating new habits and following a few simple rules, you can be the leader that God created you to be.

Most of our text will come from the first six books of the Bible. These books chronicle the Israelites' escape from Egypt, the miracles, their disobedience, God's grace, and the final descent into the land that God promised them four hundred years earlier. This guide provides solid, practical leadership strategies and combines them with the life example of Joshua.

This study guide maps a span of eight weeks. Each week contains five lessons. Each lesson will require about fifteen to twenty minutes for you to complete. You can do the homework all at once or daily, whichever works best for you. I know if there is one thing that students hate, it is homework. However, the Bible says in Proverbs 2:6, "For the Lord gives wisdom, and from His mouth come knowledge and understanding." The recipe to your knowledge and understanding comes from God's Word. So I want to help create in you a habit of daily study and spiritual growth. If you knew that ten minutes a day could change you and start you down the path of your purpose, would you give it? I primarily use the New International Version of the Bible. If you use a different translation, the verses will still mean the same thing within their context.

This study guide was written in conjunction with *A Joshua Generation*, an easy-to-read, nine-chapter book that will lay a good foundation on the same principles. It is not as in-depth a study but will certainly challenge you and guide you to develop your God-given gifts toward a heart of leadership.

In your reading, you may notice that I discuss John Maxwell and his leadership ideas several times throughout this book. I believe that Maxwell is anointed by God and has educated many through his teachings and writings. What's so valuable about his work is that he takes the Word of God and applies it to everyday life. My strategy is to take the information that I have learned through his teachings as an adult and adapt it to the younger generation of leaders that God is calling forth—and that includes you.

Don't just simply participate in this study. Make a commitment to practice these teachings. God's Word offers a blueprint that shows you how to live a life that will be pleasing and bring honor to Him. Your participation will challenge you to make a change and to begin your journey to becoming one of God's leaders.

Visit our website at www.myjoshuaproject.com to share what God is doing through this study and to purchase gear or resources from the store. Molly is available to speak to your group on many topics, including but not limited to leadership growth. She can be contacted through this site as well.

# Week One

## What Is Leadership?
### Day One

Growing up, did you ever play the game "follow the leader"? Someone was first, and everyone else followed and tried to mimic what the leader was doing. The person in the front of the line always tried to jump over things, curve and twist around, and do other stunts that might cause the followers to mess up or do something that was not the exact copy of the one leading. During my teaching career, I taught both kindergarten and fifth grade, and it didn't matter what age, the kids still fought over who was going to be the leader. Think back to your elementary school years. You probably had a system in each class that decided who was going to be line leader for the day.

What does it mean to you to be a leader? _____

_____

Simply put, a leader is one who leads. Then what does it mean to lead? I would define lead as, "to go first or to be in the front." It seems like we had it right, even as young children playing elementary games.

Who is the first person to pop into your mind when you hear the word "leader"? Throughout history, many people have been called leaders. Some are in the military, some in business, and others are called leaders because they made a contribution to their communities. But God has His own "Hall of Fame." Some of the greatest leaders who ever lived are chronicled in God's Word. In fact, God's plan is for every born-again Christian to lead others to Him.

Look up Acts 1:8 and record what Jesus tells His disciples to become.

_____

The word *witnesses* used in this verse is found in the original language as "*martys.*" It has the same meaning as our word, "*martyr.*" It is the same word used when Scripture speaks of disciples being put to death for their belief in and devotion to God (Acts 22:20). It means,

"One who declares with confidence what he himself has seen or heard." Define in your own words what it means to be a witness. _____

Now look up Daniel 12:3 and rewrite it here.

_____

_____

_____

The original King James Version says, "and those who turn many to righteousness" My NIV translation says, "who lead many to righteousness." How do I lead someone to righteousness? Would you agree with me that if you are witnessing the love of God and His goodness, then you are also leading others to righteousness? If we can agree on that, can we also agree that if God's purpose for each born-again Christian is to be "[His] witnesses in Jerusalem, and in all Judea and Samaria, and to the ends of the earth" (Acts 1:8), then it is also God's purpose and His greatest desire for you to lead all to the paths of righteousness?

We have a great mentor or one who teaches us to lead to righteousness. This word "lead" is also the same word that is used in Psalm 23. "The Lord is my shepherd; I shall not want. He maketh me to lie down in green pastures: He leadeth me beside the still waters. He restoreth my soul: He leadeth me in the paths of righteousness for His name's sake." Isn't it comforting to know that before we are expected to lead anyone in the paths of righteousness that He first will lead us?

So let's review. We know that a _____ is one who declares the love of God and what He has done and how God has changed his or her life. God also says those who witness for Him and lead others away from sin into righteousness _____ like the _____ forever and ever. To summarize the earlier verses: it is God's desire for us to _____ (starts with an "L") others to Him. And to lead means: _____.

In conclusion, if you are going to lead many people to righteousness, you first have to be righteous. But you are not expected to do it alone, because God will lead you down those paths, comforting you and restoring you along the way.

Take a minute and record what God has showed you today about who you are, what He intended for you to be, and how He defines a leader.

_____

_____

_____

_____

_____

_____

_____

_____

# What Is Leadership?
## Day Two

Yesterday we learned that God's desire is for us to be witnesses to the ends of the earth. Write what happens to those who lead others to righteousness. _____
_____
_____

In this section, let's continue this same line of study and give you some more proof that God's purpose is for you to lead. Do you still doubt that God wants *you* to be a leader? Turn in your Bible to Genesis 1 where you will find something extremely interesting.

In all of God's creations from verses 1 to 25, He spoke of, better yet, *commanded* this universe and all of its components into existence. Each day begins with a verse that states, "And God said." So He spoke, let it be, and it was. But look what God said in verse 26. "Let us make …" will become clearer as we continue to read on. Think through each word as you write Genesis 2:7 below. _____
_____
_____

Did you read anything interesting? In Genesis 1:26, God turns to His Son, and His Spirit and almost like He was consulting with them said, "Let us make man …" Then in 2:7, the Lord God put His hands in the dirt and formed man. He then breathed into his nostrils so he could live. The six previous days were days of authority and speaking life into existence, but man was so special that God handmade him with affection.

If I could offer you a choice between a bag of store-bought chocolate-chip cookies or some homemade, warm cookies directly out of the oven, which would you choose? I want to get up and bake some cookies, just thinking about it. We all love to be given something made just for us. We know how much time, care, and thought goes into a gift like that.

In verse 7 the word "form" comes from the Hebrew word *"yaw tsar,"* which is the word used to describe a potter molding a piece of clay. I perceive that God created Adam in the same frame of mind and cautious manner that a potter creates a work of art. How exciting to recognize the change in God's attitude and actions when it was time to create man.

Now let's go back to chapter 1 verse 26. Reread this verse and record why God created man. _____

Your Bible probably says "to have dominion over" or "to rule." This word derives from the exact same root word as the one in Psalm 23:3. Remember, "He leadeth me in the path of righteousness"? Well, today He created you to rule over the earth and its inhabitants or lead over the fish, birds, and all creatures that move along the ground. So in other words you were born to lead! You were created in His image to lead in His absence. Don't misunderstand that phrase, "in His absence." As Christians, we know that God is a living God, and we can talk with Him and have a personal relationship with Him. However, there are many who—because they can't see Him—believe that He is something other than their friend. They need a leader in His "absence."

God wants you to be a leader to Christians and nonbelievers alike. He gave you the authority to stand firm when others are doing things that do not please God. Some Christians aren't brave enough to stand up to their peers and lead to righteousness. But He also said you would lead or rule over the unbelievers as well.

Look up Psalm 110:2 and write where God says you will rule. _____
_____

God will even allow you to lead in the midst of your enemies. Refer to the scenario that I gave a moment ago: you are with a group of nonbelievers, and they are doing things that do not please God. Let's just say that you speak up and warn them that their behaviors are not in their best interest. Do you think you would then be standing in the midst of enemies? I have a hunch you will make an enemy or two. But God already said He would allow you to lead, and what a better place to lead for God?

Fill in the blanks as you review what you have learned in this section. You were _____ to lead (Genesis 1:26). You were created in God's _____ and you were _____-_____ with care and love. With authority, He created the earth; but with affection, He created you. You will not only lead your peers, but you will also lead in the midst of your _____. God loved you so much that He took the time to consult with

His Son and the Holy Spirit before He carefully formed you from the dust of the earth. He then breathed into your lungs to give you life that is exactly in His likeness. He created you so that you could rule the earth and be His leader in His absence. He created *you* to lead.

Reflect on this and journal a prayer to God. _____

_____

_____

_____

_____

_____

_____

# What Is Leadership?
## Day Three

We've discovered some heavy but exciting stuff in the last two days. Let's take a day just to unveil what it means for you to lead. Many people do not consider themselves as leaders, but John Maxwell gives the definition of leadership as influence.[1] So, what is influence? Define influence in your own words. _____

_____

*Webster's Dictionary* says, "A power affecting a person, thing, or course of events, especially one that operates without any direct or apparent effort." It also lists a few synonyms: "to sway, direct, control, or rule." There's that word "rule" again. Let me give you my definition of "influence." If you, because of who you are, what you say, or what you do, can cause someone else to make a decision, then you have had influence over them.

A great example of influence would be peer pressure. If someone can cause you to do something that you might not have done before, then he or she has influence over you. Or, according to John Maxwell's definition, the person leads you. When talking about peer pressure, "influence" sounds negative so let me give you some positive examples.

Have you ever heard a new CD and thought it was sent front heaven above. So you immediately call your friends and tell them this CD is a *must*! Within hours, they all have the CD and you are on the phone discussing each and every song and lyric. You have had influence on your friends. What about a new pair of shoes or jeans? My boys love sushi and have talked quite a few friends into trying raw fish for the first time. Now that's influence!

The truth is that we all influence somebody every day, all day. If you have younger siblings in the house, you are definitely being an influence. Maybe you are the youngest child but have cousins, nephews, or nieces. Believe me: they are watching your every move. Take a minute and think about this. Write down who you believe you have influence over today.

_____

_____

Everybody has influence regardless of gender, age, race, background, or intellect. Go back and read Genesis 1:28. When God said "them," who was He talking about? _____ and _____. He told them to be fruitful and increase in number; fill the earth and subdue it and _____. He told Adam and Eve, both male and female, to rule the earth.

Turn your Bible to First Timothy 4:12. Journal what that verse states. _____
_____
_____

Apparently, Timothy had some people perhaps questioning his leadership ability. Paul told him to not let anybody run over him because of his age. But he needed to set an example for the believers in everything he did. Paul knew that if he lived a righteous life, then through his actions he would eventually gain the ability to influence this group of believers.

Now read Titus 2:7–8. How does this verse tell him to set an example and to teach? _____
_____

Do you think this would be good rule for your life as well?

Let's go back to Genesis and see who else had influence in the Garden of Eden. Look at chapter 3 verse 1. Even the serpent had influence. "Now the Serpent was more crafty …" In other words, he was a creative little booger. He began to engage Eve in a harmless, playful conversation. Do not ever allow Satan to engage you in a harmless, playful conversation. Satan is the creator of lies and deception. He knows how to tell just enough of the truth so that you will be deceived into believing that it is all truth. That's why in James 4:7 God says to resist the devil.

Go back to Genesis 3 and read on through verse 6. There is something significant in this verse once Eve has eaten the fruit. Fill in these blanks: "She took some and ate it. She also gave some to her husband, _____." Things that make you go, *hmmm*. According to verse 6, Adam was with Eve during this exchange. It seems evident we have some serious influence issues. First of all, God created Adam and Eve to rule over the serpent (1:28). Adam and Eve also had a relationship as husband and wife and therefore had influence over each other. Adam was standing beside her, for goodness sakes. To put it in perspective, there is a serpent that has influence that was not given from God. There is a woman who allowed another's influence to talk her into doubting God's words. And we have a man who refused to stand up and be the leader that God destined him to be. Now, because Adam and Eve began to question the authority that God birthed in them, we all live in a cursed world.

As a review, the definition of leadership is _____. Everybody has influence regardless of _____, _____, _____, _____, or _____. Satan is the creator of _____ and _____, but he is also a creative influencer. However, God has given you the authority to lead. You do have influence over many and because of that, you are leading them. It doesn't matter if you are male, female, old, or young. You are always influencing. And most importantly, Satan wants to steal your influence. Resist the devil and be the leader that God destined you to be.

Take a minute to journal your prayer to God.

_____

_____

_____

_____

_____

_____

_____

_____

# What Is Leadership?
## Day Four

We learned enough already to know that not all influence is positive. There are plenty of negative influences these days with televisions, computers, music, magazines, and friends. What? *Friends?*

We have all been given the ability to influence and the mandate to lead. However, influence can be used for either bad or good decisions. We saw yesterday how Satan uses negative influence to trap us into sin. But men and women are both guilty of positive and negative influences. Some are conscious efforts while others are unaware.

Take your Bible and look up 1 John 3:7. Copy the first part of that verse. _____
_____

Now read Psalm 109:1–8. After reading these verses, what gives you a clue that he is a wicked "leader"? _____
_____

So according to God's words, others will lead you astray and leaders can be wicked and deceitful.

We're going to spend a few minutes in Numbers 13 so go ahead and turn your Bible there. In this passage, the children of Israel have just settled into the desert and are making a plan to begin their attack on the neighboring cities to take the land that God has promised them. God has just told Moses to get some men together for them to spy on the land. Look at the last few words in verse 2. Write down how this verse ends. _____
_____

Now, you may not have the same version as me so let me tell you what the last five words of this verse are: "send one of its leaders." So God asked Moses to choose a leader, one man from each of the twelve tribes. He reiterates their status in verse 3. "All of them were leaders of the Israelites."

So now we set the stage and we are clear that the leaders from each tribe went on a forty-day exploration to spy on this land. You know the story. Twelve went in but only two came back with good news that the Israelites could defeat the inhabitants; the other ten had a different opinion.

Now look in chapter 13 at verse 32 and record here what the first sentence says. _____
_____
_____
_____

They knew that because they were leaders in the community they had influence and the people would listen to them. They chose, however, to abuse the power of influence that God had given them.

Go back and read verse 2 again, but this time focus on the second phrase. "Send some men to explore the land of Canaan, which _____ to the Israelites." In case you missed it again with your version, let me help fill in the blanks: "… which I am giving to the Israelites." Whoa, Nellie! God sent them to spy on a land just to pick out which field they would plant in. He had already said He was giving it to them, which meant they had to do nothing in return but trust in Him.

Let's continue on to chapter 14 verse 1 through 4. After reading these verses, what did you notice that seemed significant? _____
_____

If you were to think about the number of people in this community, there may be something else that becomes a little more notable. Let me give you some background to paint a mind picture. The citizens of this nation numbered over six hundred thousand men alone, and added to that were wives and children. There were also livestock and people who had tagged along and others who had been picked up along the way. These men were the top twelve of almost 2 million people (Ex. 12:37).

Again, with this in mind, reread verses 1 and 2 and see if there is a three-letter word that jumps out at you that just seems amazing. _____ Is it just me or does it seem a little overwhelming to know that ten men in a position of leadership had the ability to persuade two million people into believing that they could not trust God to do what He had already promised to do. In fact, they were so mad at Caleb and Joshua they were even making a plan to stone them (v. 10). Do you realize the power you have been given to persuade?

When you think about your influence and whether it has been primarily a good influence or a bad one, mark where you fall on the line below.

Mostly Bad ------------------------------------------------- Mostly Good

Take a minute to go back and review. You can have both a _____ influence and a _____ influence. You have the ability to lead millions of people. You have been given a great power to _____ others. Do you always use that power to honor God?

Leadership is serious. You will give an account one day to God of how you led. If God gives you an incredible opportunity to show others the way to righteousness, be careful you point them in the right direction. With influence comes great responsibility.

If you are not sure where your influence lies, ask God to show you His perspective on your experiences. Let Him reveal in you if there are areas that may need to be cleaned up. If He reveals some instances, ask God to forgive you and redeem those times. Confess them to Him and ask Him to give you another opportunity to lead. Write what you want Him to know now.

_____

_____

_____

_____

_____

_____

_____

_____

# What Is Leadership?
## Day Five

I hope you are not feeling beat up from our study yesterday. The reason for this workbook is not to criticize you for your failures, but to teach you what God wants you to know and to celebrate your victories. However, I feel that it is very important to understand what the consequences are for a negative influence.

We will be going back to Numbers 14, but this time we are going to verses 36–38. Take a minute to read them. What emotions are you experiencing right now?_____

_____

Shock, fear, surprise? What emotions do you think Joshua and Caleb went through? _____

_____

The negative attitude of these ten leaders caused rebellion in the camp and caused bad attitudes to infect the entire community. Because of their contamination, God allowed a parallel punishment by infecting them with a deadly disease. The consequence of a negative influence is death.

Find Matthew 15:13–14. Jesus is speaking to the disciples. In these two verses, it seems like He almost talks in riddles. What is your interpretation of these two verses? _____

_____

_____

_____

For me to be able to shed a little light, you need to turn in your Bible to Isaiah 61:3. What does it say that the Lord planted for the display of His splendor? _____

_____

I know that we are doing a lot of running around but turn to Psalm 1:3 and write the definition of the righteous man as he is described as a tree. _____

_____

_____

_____

So, referring back to Matthew 15:13, can we agree that God is the planter of oaks of righteousness or men that live holy unto God? Can we then agree God did not plant an unrighteous man? So, if Matthew 15:13 says, "Every plant that my heavenly Father has not planted will be pulled up by the roots," we can expect that God will remove the weed and destroy it. What does God call these "plants" or unrighteous men in verse 14? _____ _____. So in other words, would you feel comfortable calling them a guide of the blind or a leader of the blind? Maybe it is better explained that they are leaders given to those that have not yet been born again so they may lead them to the paths of righteousness?

What point is Jesus making by telling this story? _____ _____

Death in the instance of the Israeli leaders was instant, physical death, but sometimes in our lives it could mean the death of something else. It could be the death of a relationship or the death of respect. It could be the loss of influence. And if you no longer have influence over this individual, then you have lost the ability to lead them. I cannot think of anything more devastating than not being able to fulfill your God-given destiny because you have lost influence over your appointed mission field.

Let's review today's important points. The consequence of a negative influence is _____. Jesus is the planter of the oaks of _____. Every plant that the heavenly Father has not planted will be pulled up by the _____. You have been given a power greater than any other. This power is the ability to influence people. With this power, there is great responsibility. How will you use your gift of influence?

Take a few minutes and let the magnitude of that statement settle in your spirit. There is no reason to be overwhelmed because God says in Exodus 15:13, "In your unfailing love you will lead the people you have redeemed. In your strength you will guide them to your holy dwelling." You see, He is the ultimate leader. And just as the phrase states, He will first lead you before He requires you to lead others. Journal to Him what today's study has shown you.

_____

_____

_____

_____

# Week Two

## How Do I Lead?
### Day One

Last week we learned that even young children have the ability to lead other children. You can lead whomever you have influence over. But, we also learned that you can lead positively or negatively. Great leaders also realize that influence is a powerful tool and they are grateful to God for this gift. Because they realize its value, they are very careful to learn how to use it.

I remember being excited about getting my driver's license at sixteen. I was counting the days before my birthday until I could take the test and be given permission to drive alone. I grew up in the country with plenty of back roads and pastureland so my parents, grandparents, and neighbors all gave me plenty of opportunities to practice driving long before the blessed day arrived.

What if I didn't have to take a driver's test, but was just awarded a license and keys? What if I had never gotten behind the wheel of the car before that day? How do you think that first trip would have ended up? I was thinking of the word *disastrous!* It would be the same effect if you never "learned" the skills necessary to become a great leader. Leadership is a process. Leaders are not born and developed overnight. John Maxwell puts it this way: "Leadership develops daily, not in a day."[2]

Let's go back and discuss Joshua. He was much younger than Moses and had lived in Egypt through the days of slavery. He crossed the Red Sea with the other men and women who were escaping the hand of the Pharaoh. Then, after the sin of the Israelites, Joshua wandered in circles for forty years in the desert while waiting for the sinners to die. After all this time, only then was Joshua allowed to move toward his destiny of leadership. Look up Numbers 11:28 and write down how long Joshua had been serving with Moses. _____

_____

_____

We know from last week's story that Joshua and Caleb did not yet have the influence they needed to persuade the Israelite community to take the land that God had promised. Even though both sets of leaders (Moses and Aaron and Joshua and Caleb) were begging for the will of God and for the acceptable behaviors from the people, notice the two different responses taken by these four leaders: Moses and Aaron who were much older and had more experience versus Joshua and Caleb who are not yet looked upon as influential game changers.

Read Numbers 14:5 and write what Moses and Aaron do. _____
_____

Now read Numbers 14:6–9 and jot down a few things about how Joshua and Caleb react to the situation. _____
_____
_____

Did you notice what they did differently? If so, what was it? Let me give you a hint. What did Moses and Aaron *say* to the people? _____
_____

Do you think that was the correct decision? _____ Why or why not? ___
_____

Read verse 10 and record what the Israelites response was to Joshua and Caleb's pleas. ____
_____

Joshua and Caleb had good intentions. They wanted nothing different than Moses and Aaron wanted. But Moses and Aaron were wiser and older and they knew that the situation was not going to be good. They knew that the only hope for these people was to cry out to God and intercede for God's grace. They said nothing to the people as they fell on their faces in prayer. Joshua and Caleb thought that they could persuade the people and began to tear their clothes in mourning. They reminded the people of God's promise and His faithfulness and begged the people to turn from their rebellion—an act that could have gotten them killed.

As you mature, you will use your experiences, studies, and knowledge of life to mold you into a better decision maker. Joshua waited a long time before he was ready to lead the nation into the battles that were necessary for the conquest of the land. But he continued to lead those he did have influence over, and he continued to learn from his mentor while he was waiting on God's timing.

As a review, leadership takes time. Yes, God had a plan for you before you were born, and, yes, you were created to lead, but leadership is a _____. Leadership develops _____ not in a _____. Joshua was Moses' aide since his _____.

I hope you learned from today's lesson that great leadership takes time. This doesn't mean that you cannot lead where God has placed you now, but be diligent in building knowledge while God builds your experiences; both will make you grow.

Has today's guide changed the way you have thought about how to lead? Journal to God a minute and share with Him your thoughts. Let Him know any fears and concerns that you might have. _____

_____

_____

_____

_____

_____

# How Do I Lead?
## Day Two

We are going to spend the next few days talking about the behaviors of a great leader. Joshua was mentored by Moses from a young age (Numbers 11:28). And Moses helped Joshua create some crucial lifelong habits. Joshua knew that successful leaders are learners. He followed closely behind Moses and learned from his life experiences as well. Moses modeled, while Joshua followed. His time to lead had not yet come.

We will use Exodus 33 for the next several studies, so go ahead and turn there and mark it. At this time, the tabernacle had not yet been built. So Moses constructed a temporary tent that he used when he wanted to spend time with God. Look at verse 7 and write down where Moses pitched the tent. _____
_____ Why do you think this is significant? _____
_____
_____
_____

The first behavior you must exemplify, to be the leader God called you to be, is that you must take time to get alone with God. Joshua watched Moses go into this tent and spend time one on one with God. Joshua longed to be with God and have the same experiences that Moses did. Look up Exodus 33:11 and notice what Joshua does at the tent. Write down what you discover. _____
_____
_____

Why is this important? _____
Why do you think he stayed? _____

Look up Mark 1:35 and jot down the habit that Jesus created. _____
_____
_____

_____Even Jesus needed to separate himself regularly to get alone with His Father.

Moses knew God's promise found in Proverbs 8:17. Copy it below. _____
_____

He not only knew of this promise, but he also practiced it. Look up Deuteronomy 4:29 and read where Moses reminded the people to seek God.

The second habit that is a requirement for you to become the leader that God has called you to be is that you must seek God and His heart. To seek the heart of God means that you want the same things that He loves. You want to be unified with God and so you take on His desires as your own.

Look at Exodus 33:18. What does Moses ask for? _____
_____We are going to spend more time on this later this week, but Moses wanted more of God. He wasn't content with the everyday activities if God was not with him. Read verse 11 and write down how the Lord spoke with Moses. _____
Can you imagine having daily conversations with God face-to-face? God longs for you to have an intimate relationship with Him. He wants to talk with you and He wants you to give Him the time to seek after Him and His heart.

Again, I go back to the promise in Proverbs 8:17. Look at what you wrote above. God cannot lie. If He promised you would find Him, then trust Him that you will. Read Numbers 12:6–8. Do you think Moses sought and found God? _____
Would you like God to say these words about you? _____

As we review, don't just write these words. Let them sink into your innermost being and become who you are. Successful leaders are _____. To be the leader that God has called you to be, you must take time and _____with God and you must _____ after God and His _____.

You will never be old enough or established enough to stop learning. If you are going to be great, you will learn until you die. You will never "arrive." You can do good ministry and make a little difference on your own, but you will never reach your full potential. You also will not be all that God has called you to be without a daily separation of all business and noise and an "alone" time with your Father. I also want you to think about the word "all" as in "all your heart." This doesn't mean partial, sometimes, when it is convenient, or when your friends are doing it. It means with every ounce inside you, with everything. There is nothing else that is more important than seeking God so you share the same heartbeat.

Reflect on today's lesson and journal your thoughts to Him.

_____

_____

_____

_____

_____

_____

_____

_____

# How Do I Lead?
## Day Three

I pray you learned by watching Moses and Joshua yesterday. To review again one of the most critical statements made thus far, fill in the following blanks: Successful _____ are _____. It is heartbreaking when leaders become unteachable. Remember that there is not enough time during the span of your life to learn everything you need to know.

Today we are going back to Exodus 33. I want to focus on verses 8 and 9 and give two new habits that great leaders must possess. Read verse 8 and write the action verbs that are used. What is it that the people do?

_____

The verb that I want you to pay most attention to is what they did after they "rose and stood at the entrances of their tents, _____."

If you are going to be in the front of the line, you will have people watching you. You must know this and be willing to expose yourself to others. This means exposing the victories as well as defeats. Some of these people will be encouraging you, pulling for you, and praying for strength for you. Others will be doing the exact opposite. Some will be watching and waiting for you to make a mistake. They will rejoice when you fail and will tell as many people as they can that you are not "the real thing."

The fear of making a mistake is a real stronghold in the lives of many people, young and old alike. This book is a testimony to that. I waited three years after God spoke to me to write it because of the fear of failure. So many times, God is urging us to take a step in a new direction and Satan begins to deceive us into believing that we can't do it and will never be good enough to pull it off. Well let me tell you something shocking. You can't do it alone and you will never be good enough alone. But in partnership with God the Father, the interceding of His Son, and the direction from His Holy Spirit, there is nothing you can't do!

In your lifetime, you will make mistakes and people will see them. We will talk in great detail about what to do later in this workbook, but until then admit your mistakes, ask God's forgiveness, and ask Him to redeem them. He is faithful and just to forgive us our sins and to cleanse us from all unrighteousness (1 John 1:9).

The next thing that is critical to godly leadership is found in verse 9 of Exodus 33. Copy the verse below. _____

_____

_____

Who was speaking to Moses in this verse? _____

Read verse 13 and journal what Moses asked from God. _____

_____

You must learn to listen to God and learn His ways. Moses would listen as God spoke with Him. Moses would listen carefully to everything He said and was sure to do what He asked. Moses also wanted God to teach him His ways so that he would know the heart of God. He was still seeking God's heart. The phrase "that I may know" comes from the root word *"yada,"* which means "to be revealed, to recognize, to know by experience." It is used many times in Scripture when discussing a private, intimate relationship. For example, in Genesis 4:1 "Adam lay with his wife, Eve, and she became pregnant."

To have a relationship like that means that you will know the most intimate, private details like a husband and wife know each other. Moses wanted to have this kind of relationship with God. He wanted to know the most private of God's thoughts. Moses wanted to know His heart.

Think about your relationship with God as we do today's review. All leaders at some point in their life will be _____ by others. With God's help, there is _____ you cannot do. You must learn to _____ to God and _____ His ways.

I want you to remember from today's study that *great* leaders do not walk in their own ways and desires, but they listen to God's wants and seek His plan. God wants you to have an intimate relationship with Him. He wants to tell you His thoughts and teach you His ways. Learn from Moses and mimic his actions.

What would you like to journal to God today about your relationship with Him? Ask Him how He would like your life to be different based on today's knowledge.

_____

_____

_____

_____

_____

_____

_____

_____

# How Do I Lead?
## Day Four

Yesterday we learned that successful leaders are watched by others, and if you want to give them something to talk about you need to make it a habit to listen to God and ask Him to teach you His ways. God reveals His heart to those that know Him and have an intimate relationship with Him. Today let's go one step further and talk about the persistence of Moses and his desire to see God at work.

God had already promised Moses and the Israelites that they would enter the promised land. It wasn't enough for Moses to know that he would make it there. If He did not have God directing Him, it wasn't worth the travels. Go back to Exodus 33 and look at verse 2. Who did God tell Moses He would send before the people of Israel? _____
Why did God say He would not go with them in verses 3–6? _____
_____

Why do you think Moses was not satisfied with this answer? _____
_____

Moses continued to pursue God and said to Him in verse 12, "You have been telling me, 'Lead these people,' but you have not let me know whom you will send with me." What do you think his reasons are for pressing God to know who will go with them? _____
_____
_____

God finally responds and answers Moses' prayer. Rewrite Exodus 33:14. _____
_____
_____

The word "presence" here is the Hebrew word *"paniym."* It means "the face of God." It literally means, "My face will go with you." This sentence can actually give us a glimpse of what verse 11 from earlier in the week means. "Face-to-face" has the same meaning as being in God's presence. Therefore, Moses' face was in front of God's face, or, in other words, Moses' face was in the presence of God. Successful leaders stay in the presence of

God. Moses was willing to stay behind and he would not enter into the Promised Land unless God's presence was with them.

How does Moses respond to God in verse 15? _____

_____

_____

He is still urging God to do something more. He is still not contented with the answer of God. Moses knew that they needed to be set apart from the other nations and nothing could really accomplish this except the presence of God.

Read verse 18 and write down Moses' final question to God. _____

_____

God had already agreed to Moses' urging by deciding He would go with the children of Israel. But Moses was still not satisfied. He was hungry for more of God and for a closer relationship with Him. He wanted to experience the splendor of God. To be the leader that God has called you to be, you must remain hungry for more of God. Never be satisfied with the average. Pursue Him and His presence.

Having an intimate relationship with God gave Moses boldness. Look up Exodus 3:6 and explain what Moses did and why. _____

_____

_____

Moses has become quite familiar and very comfortable with God. Before, he felt he had to hide from God. Now, he has a relationship where he felt like he could ask for anything. Even though God refused to show him, God was not angry or disappointed with Moses. He simply showed him his boundaries. How did God respond to Moses' request in verse 20 of chapter 33? _____

_____

_____

God made a compromise with Moses and called him to a private meeting on top of Mount Sinai. Verse 5 of chapter 34 says, "Then the Lord came down in the cloud and stood there with him …" Moses continued to ask God one last time to accompany them on their journey. Finally, this persistence won God's favor. God then made a covenant with Moses on behalf of the people of Israel (v. 10).

Read verses 29–35 and recount what happened to Moses and why.

_____

He had asked to see God's glory, but he was unaware that he reflected the glory of God, and he received the answer to his prayer.

In review, Moses was willing to give up the promised land unless God's _____ was with them. Successful leaders _____ in the presence of God. To be the leader that God has called you to be, you must remain _____ for more of God. Never be _____ with the average. _____ Him and His presence.

Write a prayer asking God to create a hunger in you for Him. Ask Him to help you long to stay in His presence. _____

_____

_____

_____

_____

_____

_____

# How Do I Lead?
## Day Five

Before we dive into today's study, I want to tell you how proud I am of you for hanging in there. I know we had a lot going on and many objectives that needed to be learned. I hope by the end of this week you are beginning to see yourself more as a leader and are learning the tools necessary to develop your skills.

We are finishing up this week with something that God told Moses who, therefore, taught Joshua, who passed it on to all of the children of Israel. Turn in your Bible to Exodus 17. We hear the mention of Joshua for the first time in verse 9. Joshua is fighting a battle and is unaware of what God is doing. Read the story in verses 8–15.

These events are taking place and Joshua knows nothing about what is happening on the mountain with Moses, Aaron, and Hur. Look at verse 14 and write down what God told Moses to do. _____

_____

_____

Why do you suppose God wanted Joshua to hear? _____

_____

_____

Forty years from now, all of these men fighting in this battle would be dead. Their children, who are too young to remember or not yet born, would be fighting for the inheritance that God promised. Joshua would be the only one left with influence, and there would be a time when he would need to tell the people stories to help them remember how awesome God was *and is* when they need Him. He would use these stories to not only build their faith, but to also build his faith. God felt it was important for Joshua to remember the past and God wanted him to remind the people of God's faithfulness throughout their journey.

God revealed Joshua's destiny to Moses this day. I wonder if either of the two even knew the impact of this conversation from God. I have to imagine that Moses suspected. From this passage on, when Moses is mentioned Joshua is usually named too. It is from this point that Moses became the mentor for Joshua. Joshua spent some of the most amazing days being in God's glory alongside Moses, as we learned earlier this week.

Look up Exodus 24:13–14. In verse 13, who went up on the mountain? _____. Now look at verse 14 and discover the two pronouns used as Moses gave instructions: _____ and _____. You can read on through verses 15 and 16 and see what an amazing experience that was. If you look at verse 12, you can see the reason that God called Moses to the mountain was to give him the Ten Commandments. This was the first time, before Moses became angry and broke them when he came down (Ex. 32). After reading these verses, can you agree with me that Joshua was with Moses and witnessed one of the most important events in history?

Many times God told Moses to write something down, or place something somewhere as a memorial to the children of Israel so they would remember where they had been and what God had done. As He gave instructions for the priestly garments, God required the names of the twelve tribes to be engraved on two stones and mounted on the shoulder pieces of the ephod. God said, "Aaron is to bear the names on his shoulders as a memorial" (Ex. 28:9–12 and 29). This is only one of several examples. God communicated the importance of remembering the miraculous, as well as pains and defeats. You will learn from both your victories and failures. Your character is developed not only in successes but also during the trials and battles that end in loss.

Let's wrap up by observing something that Joshua learned from this experience with Moses. Turn to Joshua 4:4–7. After reading the story, why do you think Joshua had the leaders do this? _____
_____
_____

Joshua even went into detail to tell the Israelites why they were removing stones to build a monument. He wanted them to remember to tell their children, and their children would tell their children to preserve the glory of God and mark the miracle of God for many years to come.

Meditate on these principles as we review. God wants you to _____ areas of your past and _____ others of the faithfulness of God. You will learn from both _____ and _____. It is important that you _____ the glory of God and tell of His miracles for years to come.

Ask God to remind you of times where He has provided for you and performed a miracle in your life. Write them down in a journal so that you can go back and remember and build your faith, and then testify to others to spread the good news of what God can do. What do you want to say to Him now? _____

_____

_____

_____

_____

_____

_____

_____

# Week Three

## Why Do I Lead?
## Day One

Last week we established a list of habits one must create to be the leader that God purposed for him. There is a lifestyle change that must happen to help you become who God created you to be. This week we are going to talk about the most important and the hardest feature to keep consistent.

God has a plan for your life, but sometimes it takes many years to fulfill your life's purpose. There are times we are walking a path while God is teaching. We are in a process learning to hear from and go in the direction that God is sending us. In the meantime, we must lead where God has placed us.

Look up Exodus 24:13 and write how this verse describes Joshua. _____.
This word in the original language means "to minister, to wait upon, or to serve." So in other words, this meant that Joshua was Moses' assistant. He was his servant. He ministered to Moses and served his every need. This meant cleaning, preparing his meals, washing clothes, writing what Moses dictated, or whatever Moses asked of Joshua. Let's think about it in today's world. Joshua would go to the grocery store, cook Moses' meals, clean up the kitchen, sweep, mop, vacuum, take out the trash, wash, iron, fold and put away his clothes, run errands, and respond to Moses' every request. What if that was your job? Could you do these things and do them with a good attitude? Look up Colossians 3:23. How did God say you are to work to do these minimal tasks? _____

_____

_____

_____

We know the ending of this story. We know that Joshua was one of the greatest leaders chronicled in the Bible. But what you may not have known was that Joshua was also a great servant. For what some believe was more than forty years, Joshua served Moses.

Read Matthew 20:26–28 and record verse 26._____

_____

_____

In verse 28, what does it say that Jesus came to this earth to do? _____

_____

Somehow, in today's world, we have forgotten that we were created to work and to serve God and others.

Record Galatians 5:13. _____

_____

_____.

Not only are we to serve one another, but how are we supposed to serve? _____. The sooner that you learn how to swallow your pride and serve others, the sooner God can begin to use you for the kingdom.

Joshua was leading even as a servant. The people watched him grow in wisdom and in strength. The people knew how he lived his life. They knew his habits and his character. They knew that he was the one to lead them forward. Turn to Joshua 1:16–18. After reading this, what are your thoughts about if and how Joshua had been leading while he was serving? _____

_____

_____

God wants to find out if you can be a servant of man and do so with love and excellence. Only if you can serve others with the right attitude can you be trusted to become the servant of God that He needs to fulfill His purpose.

Read the parable of the great banquet in Luke 14:7–11. What point is Jesus trying to make by telling this story? _____

_____

_____In God's world, He will exalt you when He decides the timing is right.

Let's take a minute to review what God has taught us today. If you feel like God does not have you in a leadership position yet, in the meantime you must lead _____

_____. Whatever you do, work at it with _____,
as working for the Lord and not _____. If you want to become great,
you must first become a _____.

God's desire is for you to learn to serve others and to put them first before yourself. He
says in Matthew 23:11–12, "The greatest among you will be your servant. For whoever
exalts himself will be humbled, and whoever humbles himself will be exalted." God will
never be able to use you for the reason He created you, nor will you find your destiny in
Him until you first learn to become a servant. Self-centeredness has no place in God's
kingdom. In other words, *it's not about you!*

Ask God to reveal areas in your life where you need to work at serving. Ask Him to help you
this week as you learn to become a servant. _____

_____

_____

_____

_____

_____

_____

# Why Do I Lead?
## Day Two

Have you given much more thought to your status as a servant? I hope God is teaching you some things this week that will change the way you live forever. Today we are going to continue down the path of sacrificing ourselves to rid us of all self-centeredness and let God elevate us as we learn to give to others, humbling ourselves so God can exalt us in His time.

Turn your Bible to Joshua 11:15 and copy it down below. _____
_____
_____
_____

What a wonderful declaration of Joshua's life. Can I challenge you to make this a goal in your life, to do whatever you are told and leave nothing undone? We are going to spend a great deal of time on obedience.

Record Joshua 1:7 below. _____
_____
_____
_____

What did God tell Joshua to do in order to be successful wherever he went? _____
_____

If someone asked you the formula for success, according to this Scripture what could you tell them? _____ If we were in elementary school, it might look something like this:

### God's law + Obedience = Success

It sounds easy, doesn't it? Then why isn't everybody doing it? The truth is that it is really hard to obey God all the time. What if all your friends were going to a party and He told you not to go? That one may be easily defeated. What if you really wanted to go to a particular college, buy a certain car, or date a specific boy or girl, and God told you to do something different? Could you obey Him in these instances?

If God told you to leave the country and move across the world to witness to people that don't look like you, act like you, or even talk your language, could you obey? If God told your parents to move to a different state to take a new job or work in a church, would you be happy with the change in friends, schools, and community?

Complete obedience is hard, and God knows it. This is why we must begin serving and obeying others with love. God will never be able to trust us with the big decisions if we first can't learn to obey the little things.

Let's say you were going to bake a cake. What would be the first thing you do? I hope your answer is that you would look at the directions on the back of the box to see where to start. If you baked a cake every day for months, it wouldn't be long before you would know the recipe by heart and you would not have to keep looking back at the instructions. The same is true with obeying God's rules. You will never be able to "obey all the laws" (Joshua 1:7) if you don't know the laws.

Look again at Joshua 1:8. What does God say to ensure that you will learn and remember His laws? _____

_____

_____

What do you think is meant by *"Do not* let this Book of the Law depart from your mouth"?

_____

_____

_____

Read Isaiah 59:21. After reading this verse, can you conclude anything differently? _____

_____

_____

_____

The goal is that you always want God's words in your mouth so that the words you are speaking are not your own but are His. You do not want to lose His words by neglecting them and therefore forgetting what He said. That is why God tells Joshua to meditate on them day and night. God wants him to do everything he can to keep His words close to his heart.

Let's reflect on today's study. Great success comes from _____. God will never be able to trust us with the big decisions if we first can't learn to _____ in the little things. You will never be able to obey the laws if you don't _____ the laws.

Obedience is necessary for growth. God is teaching you to obey the small things. He is also watching your attitude while you obey. Meditate on God's words daily. Remember them and tell your children and children's children and learn to live by them so that you may be successful.

Are there any areas in your life where you are not obeying God completely? Ask God to reveal them to you now and pray He will help you make better decisions. What do you want to tell Him now? _____

_____

_____

_____

_____

_____

_____

_____

_____

# Why Do I Lead?
## Day Three

We began this week's study with the importance of servanthood and God's desire for obedience. Today we are going to investigate our mandate to teach as well as model obedience.

Turn in your Bible to Matthew 5:19 and copy it below. _____
_____
_____
_____

What are the two action verbs that Jesus uses at the end of this verse that are required for a person to be called great in the kingdom of heaven? _____
_____. My version uses the words "practice" and "teach." The word "practice" here comes from the words "to do." The original *"poieo"* means "to act rightly, to do well, or to perform." It actually means to do these commands. The second word, "teach," is translated from *"didasko,"* which means "to impart instruction or to instill doctrine into one." That's a pretty basic concept as well. In other words, God is asking us to "practice what we preach." We are to teach obedience by modeling obedience.

It is also important to know that Jesus was talking to the Pharisees in this verse. They were the greatest at preaching the law, living in judgment, and making sure that they obeyed every commandment, and obeying those commandments with pride. They missed the point that God wanted to change them on the *inside,* and that He is happiest when we obey out of love and not out of competing to be the holiest.

As we fulfill our purpose to lead others, one area that we will be leading in is obedience. You will have to teach others to obey with your words and your actions. But you must be most careful to realize that not everyone is spiritually ready to obey God. And as people make mistakes, you cannot turn into the Pharisees or begin to exalt yourself and start to accuse or judge them in their sin. Look up Matthew 7:1 and copy it below. _____
_____

Now read Romans 14:10–13 and write what you think Paul wants you to take away from these verses. _____

_____

_____

The bottom line is that God is the only one who can see the heart of men. He called you to lead by example and through your words, but He didn't ask you to grade others on their performance. Remember our verse from week one in 1 Timothy 4:12? "Don't let anyone look down on you because you are young, but set an example for the believers in speech, in life, in love, in faith and in purity."

We are commanded to set an example or to teach through modeling. "To set an example" means "to lead the way, be the first, or initiate." Does any of that sound familiar? It is the same meaning that we found for "lead." Once again we have been commissioned to be a leader. The areas we are to pioneer are with our mouths and what we say, with our lives, through love and faith, and in righteousness. So if you are truly living a life of love and faith and with pure intent, you will find yourself being compassionate with others and not necessarily judging their ways. If you find yourself forming an opinion about someone or "judging" his or her motives, stop and check your heart. Make sure your motives are pure and are out of love.

Moses taught Joshua obedience by living as an example of one who obeys. He repeated the commandments to the people time and time again as a reminder and encourager. After Moses' death, Joshua mimicked his actions and led the people by his example. Look up Deuteronomy 4:1–2 and write in your own words what Moses is doing to the people. ____

_____

_____

Now turn to Deuteronomy 32:44–47 and write the main point that Moses is trying to make to the people. _____

_____

_____

Now let's move forward and take a look at Joshua for just a minute. Joshua leads the people across the Jordan River. In a few short days, they moved to the defeat of Jericho and Ai. From here, Joshua remembered Moses' words and followed his example by obeying the commandments that he had given earlier. Read Joshua 8:30–35 and paraphrase in your own words what Joshua did. _____

_____

_____

_____

Before we conclude today, we must read Deuteronomy 27:1–8. Based on what you know about both Moses and Joshua, in your opinion why did Joshua do these things? _____

_____

_____

Important principles to remember today are "whoever _____ and _____ these commandments will be called great in the kingdom of heaven." "Set an example for the believers in _____, in _____, in _____, in _____ and in _____." For "blessed are the pure in heart for they will see God" (Matt. 5:8).

God warned Moses over and over of the importance of keeping His commandments. Moses in turn reminded the children of Israel often and preached its importance to Joshua. Because of his constant urging and the example Moses set, Joshua learned to live his life by the rules God commanded. And because of Joshua's obedience, "the Lord exalted Joshua in the sight of all Israel; and they revered him all the days of his life, just as they had revered Moses" (Josh. 4:14).

What do you sense the Holy Spirit is telling you through today's study? Take a minute and journal your prayer to God.

_____

_____

_____

_____

_____

_____

_____

_____

# Why Do I Lead?
## Day Four

God requires our obedience and He promises blessings and prosperity when we obey Him (Deut. 28:1–14). However, He often has different motives when demanding our submission to Him.

There are times when you won't feel like obeying; sometimes you will not understand what God is doing and why you need to obey, but God has a plan. He is preparing you, teaching you, and testing you to determine when you will be ready to bring your work to completion. Your life now is a series of tests, and it may sadden you to hear that you will be in a string of tests for the rest of your life. But each test is moving you closer and closer to your destiny. How you respond to these tests will determine your position with Christ in the kingdom of God.

Look up these next few verses and record why in your opinion God tested the people.

Exodus 20:20 _____

Deut. 8:2 _____

Deut. 8:16 _____

God tests us in order to strengthen our faith, question our commitment, examine our hearts, or check our ability to trust Him.

I want you to study the obedience of Abraham. Let's dissect Genesis 22:1–2.

The first sentence of Genesis 22 states that God _____ Abraham. Verse two says, "Then God said, 'Take your son, your only son, Isaac, whom you love …'" God didn't just say, "Take your son." He adds effect for drama and states, "your only son." Now if that wasn't bad enough, He adds, "whom you love." What are your thoughts about this and the reason that God added this for emphasis? _____

_____

I can't say for certain, but I will tell you my opinion. We know from the biblical account of Lazarus (John 11:1–44) that Jesus loved Lazarus and his sisters very much. Verse 33 of the eleventh chapter of John tells us that when Jesus saw how sad Mary was "he was deeply moved in spirit and troubled." Verse 35 tells us that Jesus actually cried at the loss of his friend. God knew how much Abraham loved Isaac and Jesus knew the pain of losing a friend, just as God knew the pain of the death of a son. God understood the intense, difficult decision that Abraham would make to obey God's order. He knew the cost of the sacrifice. He left no room for argument. He already stated Abraham's case, "his only son," whom he loved very much.

In the remainder of verse 2, as if God has not already left enough up in the air for obedience, He tells Abraham to go to a particular place and sacrifice Isaac as a burnt offering. Now our minds automatically shut down and paint a not so bad picture of Isaac lying on an altar as Abraham raises a small steak knife over his head. But those of you who know me know that my mind refuses to let me stop there and believe the sweet, precious picture that is presented in Sunday school class (kindergartners can't handle the reality of a human sacrifice). So the only way that I know how to help you understand the severity of Abraham's decision to obey is to have you read Leviticus 1:1–9. I apologize in advance.

How do you think you would have responded to God if He asked you to obey to this degree? _____

Abraham didn't argue or waste any time. Back in verse 3 of Genesis 22, the Bible says Abraham got up _____.

There are a few more points I want you to get a hold of today, so I'll hurry through them. Look at verse 5 and write down who is going to worship and who is coming back down. _____ Abraham is already speaking in faith that he and Isaac would return. He believed that either God would provide a lamb or raise Isaac from the dead, which is quite remarkable if you read Leviticus 1.

Abraham knew that God could not lie. He also knew that God had made him a promise that had not yet been fulfilled, so in His greatness He was going to have to make a way. Read Genesis 21:12 and record the promise that God gave Abraham concerning Isaac. _____ _____ _____Look back to Genesis 17:19 for a deeper understanding.

What do you think Isaac was thinking throughout this journey? Read verse 7 of Genesis 22 before you answer this question. _____

_____

_____ I want you to realize that this is not only a test of Abraham's faith and obedience, but it is also a test of Isaac. In verse 6, Isaac symbolically carried his bundle of wood on his back just as Jesus carried His wood (cross) to be used for His sacrifice.

Although we don't know exactly how old Isaac was, we do know that Genesis 21:34 says that Abraham stayed in the land for a long time. Again in 22:1 the verse starts with, "Some time later." We do know, however, that Abraham was well over one hundred years old. Isaac could have easily fought him and overcome Abraham as he was placing him on the altar. We can only assume that Isaac voluntarily climbed onto the altar and lay down, trusting his father's faith and offering his own obedience.

God had something miraculous waiting for Abraham at the top of the mountain. Abraham could never experience the presence of God and witness the supernatural and provision of God if he had not made the decision to trust in God and obey Him, whether or not he understood the hows and whys. But greater than the effect of Abraham's obedience on himself was the experience he gave his son. What do you think Isaac learned through this encounter? Do you wonder what went through his mind?

Isaac witnessed the supernatural miracle of God our Father. He heard his father have a conversation with an angel and a second time he heard a promise from the angel concerning himself. He stood in the very presence of God and worshipped Him with his father, and was only allowed to do so because of the submission he showed after his father modeled great courage and obedience before him. On a scale of one to ten, with ten being the highest, grade yourself on your ability to obey God. _____

God often tests His children. He is preparing you for greater things. He has something supernatural for you on the mountain within His presence. What would you sacrifice to be able to witness the miracles of God? Tell Him what you are thinking now. _____

_____

_____

_____

_____

_____

# Why Do I Lead?
## Day Five

We have already discussed many of the blessings that God promised as a reward for obedience. But before we end this week, we need to discuss the warnings that God gives for disobedience.

No wonder God hates disobedience. It has been around for thousands and thousands of years. It started at the beginning of time and was the very first sin. The consequence of the disobedience of Adam and Eve was separation from the perfect, unrestricted relationship with God himself. Because of the sin of disobedience, Adam and Eve were banished from the garden. Because of the curse that Adam brought on the ground, he would forever be forced to work the ground for food and provision for his family. The consequences of this work were many hours of labor that stole his fellowship and daily walks with the Lord.

Disobedience happens to the best of us. No one is exempt, and God deals discipline as He sees fit. To set the stage of where we are going today, read Numbers 12:3 and record how Moses was described. _____

_____

God was angry with Miriam and Aaron for their jealousy and backbiting against Moses. Look at verses 6–8 and record in your own words how God Himself described Moses.

_____

_____

_____

Now that I have presented my case about what kind of man Moses was, let's take a minute and investigate his disobedience and his punishment. Turn to Numbers 20:1–12 and read the story of Moses' disobedience. In verse 8, what did God tell Moses to do? _____
In verse 11, what did Moses actually do? _____

What was the punishment that God placed on Moses and Aaron for their disobedience?

_____

_____

How do you feel about this punishment, and why? _____
_____
_____

I can almost relate with Moses. The children of Israel had been so difficult and ungrateful for so long. He had been listening to their complaining for years and finally had had enough. Regardless of the surrounding stimulus, the facts are that Moses disobeyed and God's judgment is fair. Read Deuteronomy 3:23–26 and write your thoughts. _____
_____
_____
_____
_____

God is fair and offers rewards to those who obey. He also offers consequences to those who disobey. Read Deuteronomy 28:1–14 and summarize the blessings for obedience. _____
_____
_____
_____

Now read verses 15–45 and summarize the curses that are placed on those who disobey. __
_____
_____
_____

Moses pleads with the people for the remainder of the book of Deuteronomy. He reminds them over and over of the simple promises of keeping God's commandments. Read Deuteronomy 30:15–16 and ask God to plant these words into your heart.

In review today, I challenge you to meditate on the promises of not only the blessings of obedience, but also the curses of disobedience. And remember that disobedience can cause a _____ of our relationship with God our Father. God promises _____ to those who obey as well as _____ to those in disobedience.

Are there any areas where you are not obeying God completely? Have you heard the urging of the Holy Spirit but struggled with complete obedience? Talk to God about it now. Ask Him to give you the strength to completely trust Him.

Write a commitment to Him to obey Him completely in the area where you are struggling.

I commit to: _____

_____

_____

Thank Him in advance for the blessings He will release because of your obedience in this area. Journal a prayer to Him now. _____

_____

_____

_____

_____

_____

_____

_____

# Week Four

## Who Do I Lead?
### Day One

Who do I lead? This is a vague question. In your lifetime, it is possible you will lead thousands and thousands of people. But you will never make it anywhere in life and you will never reach your God-ordained purpose if you can't first learn to lead yourself.

John Maxwell states, "No matter how gifted the leader is, his gifts will never reach their maximum potential without the application of self-discipline."[3] So what is discipline? *Webster's Dictionary* defines "discipline" as "systematic and rigorous training of the mental, moral, and physical powers by instruction and exercise."[4] In other words, being disciplined is to have control over a certain area that could easily get out of control. So how would you describe *self*-discipline in your own words? _____

_____

_____

There are many areas in our lives that need discipline. As children, we rely on our parents, teachers, and other adults to help us with discipline. However, continual adult discipline is for the immature and the same is true in your spiritual life. Before, you relied on the help of spiritual adults in your life, but it's time that you begin to mature on your own and you must begin disciplining yourself.

Last week we talked about Moses' disobedience and how it kept him from enjoying the land that God prepared for His followers. The disobedience that Moses displayed was a result of the lack of discipline. Let's go back to Numbers 20:1–13 and research it again.

In verse 8, God tells Moses to take the staff but to speak to the rock. In verse 11, Moses raises his arms and strikes the rock twice with his staff. Let's dig a little deeper to help our flesh justify Moses' frustration. Because of the wording in this chapter, many people are convinced that this is the fortieth year of Israel's travels. Several believe that these were the children of those who were punished to die in the desert. Look at verse 1 of chapter

20. No year is given where it says, "In the first month." What was the name of the place where they stayed? _____ As you continue reading the verse, write down who died and was buried here. _____

Now jump to chapter 20 verse 22. The whole community set out from where? _____ In verse 24–26, who is God preparing to die? _____ One last time, jump to 33:37–39. What was the month given that Aaron died? _____ Do you remember that it was the first month when Moses struck the rock? With this information, we can conclude that just four months passed between the time of Moses' disobedience and it was all done within the last few months as God was preparing the Israelites to take the land as their inheritance.

Knowing these details, why do you think Moses was so angry with these people for their complaints? _____

_____

_____

If you look at both sides of the story, why do you think God judged Moses so harshly for his actions? _____

_____

It is easily understood why Moses got angry, but while God does not punish anger, He will punish the sin that comes from anger. Flip your Bible to Ephesians 4:26 and write down what God says not to do when you're angry. _____

_____

God is looking for men and women who can keep control in the midst of all kinds of circumstances. He needs those that can control their behaviors when others can't. He is desperate for leaders who will remain quiet when God says to be quiet, and who will speak when He says for them to speak. Self-discipline is the outward expression of an inward truth.

Have you ever heard the expression "garbage in, garbage out"? A disciplined person is the proof of someone who has an obedient heart. Someone who is controlled on the inside will also be controlled on the outside. God will never be able to control your life fully if you don't control yourself. The only way to practice self-control is to surrender yourself to God, and let Him take control over the areas in your life that have gotten out of control.

In conclusion, before you can lead anyone else, you must learn to _____ yourself. No matter how gifted the leader is, his or her gifts will never reach their maximum potential without the application of _____ - _____. Moses' disobedience was a result of the lack of _____. Self-discipline is the outward _____ of an inward _____.

In what areas do you feel the Holy Spirit is leading you to work on self-discipline? _____

_____

_____

_____

Go to Him now and ask Him to help put your life in order, according to how He wants it, and to help you develop self-control.

_____

_____

_____

_____

_____

_____

_____

_____

_____

# Who Do I Lead?
## Day Two

Yesterday we discussed that leaders are self-disciplined. Self-discipline not only means to control yourself to behave better, but it also means doing things you may not necessarily want or like to do. But you do them because it is what you need to do. It is true that without the practice of restraint, many people get in the way of what God is doing. But it is also true that God is looking for someone who will not be controlled by his or her emotions or feelings but will be disciplined to do what is right regardless of the distractions. Today we are going to look at why it is important to be disciplined.

God expects us to apply self-discipline to the areas in our life that can keep us camouflaged with other people's lifestyles. Let me show you what I mean. Turn in your Bible to Leviticus 20 and look at verse 24. Write down the last sentence of this verse. _____

_____

_____

The NIV version uses the words "set apart." The King James Version says, "Have separated you from other people." In your opinion, what does it mean to be "set apart"? _____

_____

_____

_____

The original translation means "to divide, to make distinction, or to separate from things previously mixed together." It is the same word that is used throughout the first book of the Bible as God is creating our universe. Genesis 1:4 says, "God divided the light from the darkness." He uses it again in verses 6, 7, 14, and 18. In the same sense where God divides the day from the night (v. 14), He is also making a division between you and the world. Francis Chan believes that "Something is wrong when our lives make sense to unbelievers."[5] There should be a visible difference. Disciplined people are set apart. You have been reserved for a particular purpose, and because of your purpose you should discipline yourself to be different from others, which will cause you to be noticed. However, it is important to know that you cannot be set apart unless you are disciplined.

Look up 2 Corinthians 6:14–16 and read it to yourself. What message do you think Paul is trying to get across to the church in Corinth? _____

_____

_____

Continue to read the remainder of chapter 6, verses 17 and 18. What is your explanation of these two verses? _____

_____

To understand the meaning of 6:14 you need to read Deuteronomy 22:10. Why do you think this is important? _____

_____Basically, this just means that you should not join two things that were not meant to be joined. In other words, God did not intend for the Christian to be joined together with the unbeliever, therefore He set you aside for a special purpose. His desire is for you to be different from everyone else.

Paul does not suggest that the believer should never associate with the unbeliever. He makes this clear in 1 Corinthians 5:9–11. But where it becomes an issue is if the influence has shifted from you, the believer, to the world, the unbeliever. In other words, if the world is influencing you instead of you having influence over the world, then there has been a shift of influence. Remember the warning given in Romans 12:2. Do not conform to this world.

Copy 1 Corinthians 15:33. _____

_____

_____

You may think you are strong enough to be that positive influence in the midst of a corrupt world, but if you are truly wise you will heed the warnings of the Scripture. Remember, you want a mind like Christ, so what Christ sees as holy you should see as holy and what Christ sees as ungodly influence you should see as ungodly associations.

So a summary of these five verses in 2 Corinthians 6:14–18 would be that there are some things that do not mix; they just do not have anything in common. You are like oil and water. You do not mix, so come out from among them and be set apart.

In review of today, we must be disciplined because disciplined people are
_____. Do not be misled; bad company corrupts good
_____ (1 Cor. 15:33).

God desires for you to dedicate yourself fully to Him. You must discipline yourself to become holy. People who are holy are different and God called us to be different. Galatians 1:15 says, "But when God, who set me apart from birth and called me by His grace …" His greatest desire for you was to be different from the world so you can be more like Him.

What do you hear the Holy Spirit prompting you to say right now? Journal your prayer to God now and ask Him to help you break the yoke where you are unequally bound.

_____

_____

_____

_____

_____

_____

_____

# Who Do I Lead?
## Day Three

Today we are going to take a very easy concept and explain it thoroughly so that you have a clear understanding of self-discipline. Sometimes we have a pretty picture painted into our minds and it is difficult for us to move beyond our preconceived ideas to discover the real concept that God has for us. So let's take a minute to break down the word "self-discipline."

Self is defined as an individual's consciousness of his own identity or being. We regularly refer to ourselves as "me," "myself," and "I." We already defined discipline as continual mental, moral, and physical training. By reading the above definitions, combine them and write your meaning of the word "self-discipline." _____
_____

There is a reason it is called *self-discipline.* This is a discipline that cannot be administered by anyone else other than you.

Record Job 5:17. _____
_____

Now look up Psalm 94:12 and record it. _____
_____

According to these verses, God disciplines His children and they are blessed that He cares enough to teach them His ways. Proverbs even says that God disciplines out of love. "My son, do not despise the Lord's discipline and do not resent His rebuke, because the Lord disciplines those He loves, as a father the son He delights in" (Prov. 3:11–12).

God also commands parents to discipline their children. In Proverbs 13:24, Solomon says, "He who spares the rod hates his son, but he who loves him is careful to discipline him." See what he says in Proverbs 19:18. Rewrite it here. _____
_____
_____

You are at a place in your life where God is calling you to grow up and take responsibility for yourself. He disciplines and requires parents to discipline, but He longs for you to mature and to begin a lifetime of self-discipline. Copy 1 Thessalonians 4:4. _____

_____

_____

There comes a time when mom and dad can't make decisions for you. Men and women who God has placed in your life will not always be there to help you make wise choices.

When Joshua and Caleb returned with the other ten men who spied on the land, they had to make a choice on how they would use their influence. Joshua couldn't ask Moses and wait on his response before making his decision. There are times when God is preparing you for something big. He needs you to demonstrate self-control in little areas throughout life so that when He needs you to demonstrated areas of self-control in the crucial times, you will be ready. The best way for me to explain it is to use the illustration of a football game. Players practice long, hard hours in the heat and inflict large amounts of pain and suffering on themselves. They do this so that if they are needed to play the entire ball game, all sixty minutes of full body contact, their bodies are conditioned and can handle these requirements.

The same was true with Joshua and the children of Israel. God was teaching them self-control while preparing them for major battles ahead. Read the story of their battle at Jericho in Joshua 6. Look at chapter 6 verse 10 and write what Joshua tells the people to do or in other words not to do. _____

_____

_____

So to make it easier for you to put into perspective, let me review. The Israelites were told to march around an entire city once a day for six days and then to march around seven times on the seventh day. Many people believe that Jericho was not a very large city and the population was only a few thousand. This may be true; however, Joshua 6:7 says that Joshua ordered "the people," which translates to the "nation." So we can believe that two million people marched around a city (however big or small it was still a city) thirteen times without saying one word. They did not stop to go to the bathroom, to run through a drive-through, or rest their weary feet. They had no weapons except seven trumpets. I wonder what the people were thinking for these seven days. The only thing they could see was a massive wall separating them from the promise of God. The people of Israel were vulnerable and helpless. They could have easily been attacked from atop the wall while they circled unarmed below. This feat required self-discipline.

Self-discipline is called this because it is a type of training that cannot be administered by anyone else other than _____. God longs for you to mature and live a lifetime of _____. God is asking you to discipline the small areas in life so that you can be ready when He needs you to be self-controlled in the critical areas.

As you are growing and maturing spiritually, take responsibility for yourself and begin to practice the discipline of self-control. Ask Him to teach you how to become more self-controlled. _____

_____

_____

_____

_____

_____

_____

# Who Do I Lead?
## Day Four

Self-discipline is a requirement from every great leader. It requires you to be motivated and obedient and to have determination and patience. But discipline also requires a great amount of courage. When Joshua and Caleb returned from spying out the land, they needed courage to stand against the other leaders and report what they knew God was going to do.

A true leader not only recognizes when someone is not living a life of holiness, but he or she will also stand up for what is right and confront sin. You are different. Things that make others laugh will grieve you at the thought of the filth. Places they like to go do not excite you, and movies that they watch will make you feel uncomfortable. What makes you different? The Holy Spirit resides inside you and He doesn't like the things of this world. His focus is on spiritual things and the purpose of God for your life.

It takes courage and the practice of self-discipline to be strong and faithful. I want to teach you something most important. Your focus needs to remain on Jesus Christ, His calling in your life and that alone. Do not get consumed with whether or not you are liked by others. Do not worry about who you may need or not need to help accomplish your goals. Forget who may get offended if you tell them the truth. Do not misunderstand what I am saying. Your first commandment is to love the Lord God and to love your neighbor as yourself. Everything must be done in love; no ifs, ands, or buts.

I do want you to realize, however, that you do not need people. They need you. They are desperate for you. They depend on your leadership. Keep the influence where God intended it to be. Philippians 1:6 tells us that "He who began a good work in you will carry it on to completion until the day of Jesus Christ."

God is God, the beginning and the end. He owns everything and has a master plan. What a privilege that He has decided to use you to complete His plan. But do you realize that He doesn't need you to finish His work? You need to understand that the people you are afraid to offend are not your friends. They do not care about your feelings or how living a blatant life of unrighteousness will offend your God. Not everyone will go to heaven. Rewrite Matthew 7:13–14. _____

_____

_____

How does God say you will recognize the true sinner in Matthew 12:33? _____

_____

It takes courage to stand up in the face of sin, but it takes more discipline to correct out of love. Keep your focus on the characteristics of God that are the fruits of the spirit listed in Galatians 5:22. List them here. _____

_____

_____

Read what Paul says in 2 Timothy 2:22–26. He tells Timothy to flee from certain things, to pursue things of God, and to avoid all arguments. How is the Lord's servant supposed to approach those who oppose him? _____
A great leader will find the balance between tolerating ungodliness and confronting sin. The answer to this dilemma is that you confront not to embarrass, punish, or boast but to teach and show others the way to righteousness.

Let's turn to Joshua 7:19 and note how Joshua confronts sin in the camp. In your opinion, what is Joshua's temperament as he confronts Achan? _____

_____

Achan's sin caused defeat to the Israelite army and thirty-six men lost their lives (Josh. 7:5). Achan caused confusion and doubt to enter into the unity of people. He disobeyed God and the entire community was punished. Joshua addressed him as "son." He spoke gently, praising God in a fatherly tone. This is a perfect example of confronting in love. Joshua had compassion and his focus was not to embarrass but to help restore the children of Israel to a flawless relationship with God. He remained self-controlled and focused to carry out God's business.

In review, self-discipline requires _____. God requires us to stand up to and confront sin, but we are to do it in _____. You will recognize a tree by its _____. You should confront not to embarrass or boast but to teach and show others the _____ to _____.

2 Peter 1:3–7 says, "His divine power has given us everything we need for life and godliness through our knowledge of him … For this very reason, make every effort to add to your faith goodness; and to goodness, knowledge; and to knowledge, self-control; and to self-control, perseverance; and to perseverance, godliness; and to godliness, brotherly kindness; and to brotherly kindness, love."

Lord God, give us the greatest measure of self-discipline, which is restraint. Teach us to love. Ask for God's help in the area you need it most. _____

_____

_____

_____

_____

_____

_____

# Who Do I Lead?
## Day Five

Yesterday we talked some about restraint and the ability to discipline ourselves to allow the Holy Spirit to work and speak through us. Sometimes we want to do things our way. We want to control the situation instead of releasing it to God for Him to use as He pleases. Trust in God requires a lifestyle of self-discipline.

Look back at a Scripture that we previously discussed, Numbers 20. Read verse 12 and list the two reasons God said that Moses and Aaron could not enter the Promised Land. _____
_____

Why do you think God accused them of not trusting Him? _____
_____

Turn to Exodus 17:1–6 and write how God used Moses to bring water to the people. _____
_____

Compare the two events. What did God tell Moses to do differently at each time? _____
_____

Sometimes we expect God to do the same thing the same way. We don't trust Him with change. He may be testing our listening skills, or He may be testing our obedience. Either way, He is strengthening our discipline habits. It takes discipline to completely surrender everything to God and let Him do it His way. He wants us to remove any preconceived ideas of how and when He should perform and trust Him in His timing. Sometimes we take matters into our own hands.

Turn in your Bible to Exodus 24 and let's discuss a group of people who did not trust in God and who did not apply the discipline of self-control. What instructions did Moses give the elders in 24:14? _____ If you had been told this would, you have assumed that Moses was going to return? _____ Now look at 32:1 and write what the people said to Aaron about Moses' return. _____
_____How long had Moses been

gone? (Ex. 24:18) _____ The NIV version says in 32:25, "Moses saw that the people were running wild and that Aaron had let them get out of control …"

How quickly the people lost trust in Moses and in God. He was gone just a short time and they lost all self-discipline and disobeyed God in the vilest way. Read Exodus 14:31 and write why the people put their trust in God and Moses. _____

_____

Skip to Exodus 19:9 and list what God did so the people would be able to trust Moses.

_____

In the first verse, the people saw the power of God. In the second, they heard His voice. Discipline is developed when we can continue to trust in something that we cannot see or hear. Sometimes when we think that God is not hearing our prayers or working in our situation, our trust in Him and our discipline are being tested. The children of Israel were the seeds that Jesus was teaching about in Luke 8:13. Rewrite this verse in your own words.

_____

_____

To review, remember that _____ requires a lifestyle of self-discipline. It takes discipline to completely _____ everything to Christ and to let Him do it His way. Discipline is developed when we can continue to trust God even though we may not be able to _____ or _____ Him working in our lives.

I pray that you develop a disciplined life so that you will not be a seed that believes for a while but falls away in a time of testing. Psalm 9:10 states, "Those who know your name will trust in you, for you, Lord, have never forsaken those who seek you."

Ask God to help you continue to trust Him even when you don't feel like He is working in your life. Release control over your life to Him now and surrender your ideas of how He should do things. Allow Him to teach you trust in Him through discipline.

_____

_____

_____

_____

_____

# Week Five

## I'm Afraid to Lead
## Day One

You can embrace your calling as a leader, have all the self-discipline to succeed, know and obey all the laws, and then one day it will be your time. Even with all the studying and expectations, you will most likely be scared to death. Joshua had been the "coach in waiting" for forty years and he was terrified.

As Moses was preparing for his death, he called Joshua in front of the whole community and commissioned him to lead the people in his absence. Read Deuteronomy 31:1–8 and write down how many times Moses told Joshua to be courageous and to not be afraid.

_____

Skip to Deuteronomy 31:23 and write down the first thing that the Lord Himself tells Joshua. _____

_____

Why do you think Moses and God both told Joshua four separate times in just twenty-three verses to be courageous or to not be afraid? _____

_____

It is clear that Joshua was either afraid or going to be afraid at some point. Why do you think he was afraid? _____

_____

When you think about areas where God has placed you to lead, are you afraid? What are you afraid of? _____

_____

I imagine some of you are afraid of failure. You may feel like there is nothing worse than failing with a crowd of people following. Some of you may be afraid that no one will follow, or maybe you will miss God and not hear Him completely and you will end up going in the wrong direction. Some of you may be afraid that you will be rejected and everyone will laugh at you or isolate you.

Copy 2 Timothy 1:7. _____

_____

_____

The words "sound mind" are translated in some biblical versions as "self-discipline." We spent all of last week discussing that God would help us with self-control. He confirmed it again to us in this verse. The words "spirit of fear" are translated in the original language to "spirit of timidity." This means to be timid, shy, or cowardly, which is a weakness. Paul was speaking to Timothy's lack of confidence in himself. So in other words, God did not create you with any weakness but with the power, love, and strength that cast out all insecurities.

If the spirit of fear did not come from God, then from whom did it come? You guessed it. Satan wants you to believe that you can't do it and that you are not good enough. Actually, he is correct in one sense. You can't do it alone, and you will never be good enough by yourself. God made a promise to Joshua in chapter 1 verse 5. Copy it below. _____

_____

_____

God also takes a minute to address the fear that Joshua had with the other nations and armies that he would be fighting. Joshua was afraid of men and the power that they held over him. He was afraid of what they could do to him and the Israelites.

What is God's promise to us in Hebrews 13:6? The Lord is my _____;
I will not be _____. What can _____ do to me?

God promises that no one can stand against you (Joshua 1:5), and that He is our helper. Paul says it this way in Romans 8:31: "What, then, shall we say in response to this? If God is for us, who can be against us?"

It is okay that you are feeling some fear. The greatest leaders felt it as well. But you cannot live in that fear. Review what God has showed you today. According to 2 Timothy 1:7, God has equipped you with three things instead of fear. List them. _____,

_____, _____. God also promised Joshua, "As I

was with Moses, so I will be with you; I will never _____ you nor _____ you."

It is scary to know that God has called you to be set apart and to be an influence in the lives of others. That responsibility feels heavy, but there is nothing that our God cannot do. He promises that you will never have to do it alone. He will be your help and there is nothing that man can do about it.

Take a minute to share your fears with God. Ask Him to help you to be strong and courageous when He needs you. _____

_____

_____

_____

_____

_____

_____

_____

# I'm Afraid to Lead
## Day Two

God promises us that He has everything under control, but it's hard to remember those promises sometimes. You have a choice to make. You can give up and run in fear or you can build your faith, trust in God, and move forward. How did we say Joshua and Moses built the faith of the children of Israel? If you need a reminder from our past weeks, go back and read Exodus 17:14 and Joshua 4:1–7. _____

_____

Do you remember the leaders that were sent as spies? God had already given them a promise of land, but they were afraid of what they saw: the big people and strong cities. Look up Numbers 13:28 and write down what they said about the land. _____

_____

_____

_____

Fear has a way of changing your perspective. It is one of Satan's tricks to get us to doubt what we know God has told us. Just like we have discussed in the past, Satan begins with a little deception and then we believe a lie. Before we continue on with the wrong perspective of the land, we need to be clear on God's perspective. Turn to Deuteronomy 11:24–25 and write down what God promised the children of Israel. _____

_____

_____

Let's spend a few minutes discovering how the perspective changed with the spies in Numbers 13:26–14:4.

In verse 27, they confirm the promise that God had already made to them. "It does flow with milk and honey!" ("So I have come down to rescue them from the hand of the Egyptians and to bring them up out of that land into a good and spacious land, a land flowing with milk and honey" (Ex. 3:8). Then there is a problem. Write down the first word in Numbers 13:28. _____ Let me make a side note. If God has given you a promise, you don't need to follow it with a "but" or "nevertheless."

In Numbers 13:28, they reported that the people are powerful and the cities are fortified and large. The word "fortified" means that the walls were made strong and were created to sustain an attack. After a few minutes of debate with Caleb, the other leaders' perspectives began to change and they began to exaggerate what they experienced. Write down how they described the land in 13:32. _____

_____

_____How did they describe themselves compared to the other people in 13:33? _____

_____

_____

Can you see that when their perspectives changed they began to exaggerate and to evoke their fear into those listening? After a while, their fear and the fear in the community began to cause them to cast blame on God Himself. Read Numbers 14:3–4 and write in your own words how the Israelites blamed God. _____

_____

_____

After they changed their perspectives from God's view to their own, they blew the truth out of proportion to evoke fear and then blamed God. Finally, they began to look for a new leader. Write down Numbers 14:4. _____

_____

_____

_____

They began to take back their slavery mentality. They would rather be in bondage to man and fear than trust in God and to see the task before them through His perspective. They communicated that they did not want God's promise, His plan, or His leaders. They wanted nothing to do with God and were clear about it. It looked as though they were rejecting Moses, but in reality they were rejecting God.

There may be a time when you will try to lead others in the ways of God, but they will reject your leadership. Remember that they are not rejecting you but are rejecting God. Many people would prefer to revert back to their bondage and misery than to follow God in faith to the place of the unknown that is full of His promises and their destiny. God will fulfill His plan with or without His current people. Just be patient and God will send you a new generation of people who are willing to follow after Him.

Remember _____ has a way of changing your perspective. After the Israelites' perspectives changed, they began to _____ the truth, which evoked _____ in the people and caused them to cast _____ on God. You may be rejected as a leader, but remember people are not rejecting you but are rejecting _____.

Go back and read Deuteronomy 11:18–21. Ask God to teach you how to make a habit of learning His laws and promises so that you can build your faith and keep His perspective in fearful times. _____

_____

_____

_____

_____

_____

_____

_____

_____

# I'm Afraid to Lead
## Day Three

There are many reasons why fear can creep into our lives. Sometimes your reasons to fear may even be justified. Look at Deuteronomy 31:16–18 and then write down some reasons that Joshua would have to be afraid. _____

_____

_____

How do you think you would feel if God called you to lead a group of people, and then He told you that they were going to rebel, turn their backs on Him, and act like fools?

_____

_____

Let me ask you a question. Have you ever been with a group of people who deserted God, turned their backs on Him, and acted like fools? Every one of you who answers that question will most likely answer with a resounding "Yes." These people are the ones who are most desperate for a leader.

You may feel like sometimes your fear is reasonable, that you are justified to be afraid of God's calling on your life. According to the previous verses, I could empathize with Joshua and express he had realistic concerns. I want to teach you something about fear. In the Bible, there are thirty-five different translations or different meanings within the context of Scripture for the word "fear," but God tells us 365 times to "fear not" or "be of good courage." That's one verse for every single day of the year. Can we agree that fear must be a widespread epidemic? Regardless of the cause or the substance of our fear, God doesn't want us to do it.

In the English language, we have many different definitions for the word "fear" as well. One of those definitions is "concern or anxiety." In other words, we are anxious or worry about things and are afraid of the outcome. For example, if your car is low on gas and you are trying to make it to the nearest exit, you may be worried that you will run out of gas. In other words, you are afraid that you may be stranded on the side of the road because you do not have enough gas to get to your destination. Again, you may worry about taking a test because you are afraid that you will not do well on it.

We worry about the things of life because we are afraid that we may not get the outcome that we want. We worry about which job, which college, our spouse, our kids, our bills, our health, and many other things. But God speaks about this type of fear, this worry and anxiety that are present every day. Look up Philippians 4:6–7 and write these verses in your own words here. _____

_____

_____

_____

What do you think he meant by "the peace of God which transcends all understanding"?

_____

_____

_____

These verses tell you to turn to God in prayer daily about all the little things that you worry and have anxiety over. Once you surrender them to God, His peace will cover you and protect your hearts and minds from any attacks of Satan, and it will be such that your human mind cannot comprehend it.

Not only will His peace cover you, but He promises in Psalm 55:22 to never let you fall. Copy the promise from God when you cast your cares on Him. _____

_____

_____. What does it mean when He says that He will "sustain" you? _____

_____

There are a few things I want you to notice in the above verses (Phil. 4:6–7, Ps. 55:22). God says that He will give us His peace and will protect our hearts and minds. He also says that He will take care of us and not let us fall. However, what He does not say is that He will take our problems away. What He wants us to learn is to come to Him with them. This is another one of those testing times. He wants to teach us that it is sin for us to continue to worry and fret over daily concerns. He is teaching us to relinquish the control that we have over our lives and turn it over (cast our cares) to Him. If we hold on to our problems, then we have communicated to God that we either don't trust Him with them, or we think that we do not need His help. Write down our final promise for today, which is found in Psalm 37:5-6.

_____

_____

_____

Sometimes we _____ our fears and think they are reasonable. Another definition of fear is _____ or anxiety. God will give you a peace and will protect your hearts and minds, however, He did not say that He would _____. What a great promise He gives that if we commit our way unto the Lord and trust in Him, then He _____.

When we allow our fears to rule us, we make fear more powerful than God. Is there a task God wants you to do, but fear is holding you back? Ask Him to teach you to cast your fears on Him and reveal His promises from today's verses in your life. _____

_____

_____

_____

_____

_____

_____

_____

# I'm Afraid to Lead
## Day Four

For the past several days, we have dealt with different kinds of fears. We have discovered that all leaders have fears and it is natural to be afraid, but God wants us to learn to depend on Him under all circumstances. Today we are going to discover an additional reason why God asks us to cast our fears on Him. Look up and write down 1 Peter 5:7. _____ _____Which one of your worries did God say to give to Him? _____ Why does God want you to release your worries and give them to Him? _____ _____

The original Greek says, "It matters to Him about you." You matter to God. He cares about every one of your fears and concerns. He doesn't want you to carry the weight of these fears because He wants 100 percent of your mind and heart. He wants nothing to be a distraction and separate you from Him. You are His favorite. He loves and knows everything about you. Look up Matthew 10:29–31. What makes you different from these birds that God loves? _____ _____ _____

Flip back a few chapters to Matthew 6:25–34 and summarize them in your own words.
_____
_____
_____

God is your biggest fan and He knows everything about you down to the most shocking detail. If He knows when the sparrows fall from the trees and He knows how many hairs are on your head, can we trust that He cares enough to handle of all of our worries? To continue to worry and fear is prideful and arrogant. Copy 1 Peter 5:6. _____
_____
_____
_____

Why do you think Peter tells you to humble yourself and then follows this request with "Give God all things that burden you"? _____

_____

Humility is vital to our relationship with God. He will have no place for pride. In verse 5, He says, "God opposes the proud but gives grace to the humble." Pride and grace are contrary, or they are in conflict with each other. Pride draws us into living independently of God, where grace keeps us living at the feet of God.

God wants to hide you under His hand to protect you from the enemy's plan to devour and destroy you (1 Peter 5:8). If we will humble ourselves to Him and submit to His plan, He and only He knows the "due time." He knows the exact timing when to act and when your worries will be no more. These too are tests from God.

Your ability to stop worrying and controlling a situation and to "cast your cares upon Him" is the indication of true humility. When God has already promised to take care of our problems then it becomes pride when we refuse to give them to Him. God cares about you. He is interested in the things of your life. He wants you to be whole. He knows that worry and fear are like a cancer that will eat away at your heart, your mind, and your spirit. They will occupy your every thought and dictate your actions. He is concerned about your welfare. He already paid the price; there is no reason for you to try to pay it again.

We have a loving Father who wants nothing more than to see us succeed. He wants us to have joy everlasting. He wants to handle our problems while He teaches us to be humble. We will never be able to take care of these things in our own strength. They become a distraction to us from our purpose in God. We must stand firm and hold on to the promises of God and trust completely in Him. Look up Hebrews 13:6 and write God's promise below. _____

_____

_____

God said to cast _____ our cares on Him. He wants you to trust Him because you _____ to God. To continue to worry and fear is _____ and _____. Pride draws us into living in _____ of God, where _____ keeps us living at the feet of God. On a scale of one to ten, where do you see yourself when it comes to totally trusting in God with your worries? _____

What do feel like the Holy Spirit is saying to you today? Tell God about your fears. He cares about them and wants you to give them to Him. _____

_____

_____

_____

_____

_____

_____

_____

# I'm Afraid to Lead
## Day Five

On this final day, I want to take some time to dissect the meaning of the "fear of God." It is a term that is easily misunderstood and misused. God does require that you fear Him. Read Deuteronomy 10:12–13. List the five things that God asks of us.

1. _____
2. _____
3. _____
4. _____
5. _____

Write what you think the fear of God means in your own words. _____
_____

God does not want us to be afraid of Him. He wants to be our friend, our father, and our lover. When the "fear" in the above verse is translated, it means "to stand in awe of, to reverence, to honor, to respect." God is longing for our love. He wants us to love Him so much that we respect and reverence Him. The fear of God comes when we realize who He really is. It amazes me enough to know that He knows the number of hairs on my head, but have you ever thought about the one who could actually count those hairs? He is so awesome that He not only cares about my worries, but He already knows them and allows them for my growth.

When you begin to think about the sin that has been in your past and to grasp the realization that He forgave you and continues to love you in spite of those things, you catch a glimpse of grace and mercy. As you begin to ponder these things, you can't help but to stand in awe of Him and His goodness. Once you imagine the punishment that you deserve for your filthy sins and remember that His Son gave Himself as a human sacrifice and suffered an unimaginable death, you begin to recognize who He is and how deep His love goes. Once we begin to see who He is and what He has done and continues to do for us, we begin to gain a clearer understanding of ourselves and we start to respect and honor Him and His unfailing love. With every little step we take as we move closer to knowing Him, we move closer to fearing Him.

Copy down 1 John 4:18. _____

_____

_____

This verse actually means that we do not hide in fear of God's judgment because our genuine love for Christ confirms in us our salvation. God wants us to follow Him out of our love for Him. There are many people who have a relationship with God based on guilt for the fear that He will judge them and send them to hell. But God wants our relationship to be made perfect in love, meaning that we obey, serve, and fear Him out of love.

Record God's promise to those who fear Him, which is found in Psalm 25:12–14. _____

_____

Psalm 111:10 says, "The fear of the Lord is the _____."

When you truly fear God, then you will ask yourself these questions as you travel through life: What would God have me do in this situation? Would God be pleased with that decision? Would I watch this movie, listen to this song, or have this conversation if Jesus was sitting here next to me? The fear of the Lord is the first step to being "set apart." Because of your love and respect for Him, you will refuse to be just like everyone else.

Proverbs 2:1–4 says, "My son, if you accept my words and store up my commands within you, turning your ear to wisdom and applying your heart to understanding, and if you call out for insight and cry aloud for understanding, and if you look for it as for silver and search for it as for hidden treasure ..." Finish this passage by copying verse 5 of Proverbs 2. _____

_____

Go back and read over this again. How will you understand the fear of the Lord? _____

_____

The Bible says you will also find the knowledge of God. For several weeks we have been studying how to know God, how to know His heart, His will, and His purpose for your life. The key to knowing God intimately is to fear Him. You must first accept His words and commands. This brings wisdom, which gives understanding of the fear of God, and there you will find Him.

God does not want us to be afraid of Him but to fear Him. The fear of God comes when we _____ who He really is. We do not hide in fear of God's _____ because our love for Him confirms our salvation. The fear of the Lord is the _____ of all _____.

Pray today that He will help show you who He really is and how much He deserves all your respect. Ask Him to teach you to fear Him with a reverent fear. _____

_____

_____

_____

_____

_____

_____

_____

# Week Six

## What Is My character?
### Day One

Have you ever thought about what the word "character" actually means? Dictionary.com defines it as "the combination of traits and qualities distinguishing the individual nature of a person or thing."[6] I had to stop and ponder the words "individual nature of a person" when I first read this meaning. This definition also implies that many traits are combined to make up one's character. This means all qualities—positive and negative. Jot to the side, out in the margin, how you would describe your character.

Genesis 1:26 states that we were created in God's image. We were created to mirror God. When others look at us, they should see a reflection of God Himself. Look up Matthew 5:48 and record it. _____

_____.

We are told to be like our heavenly Father. The word used in my translation is "perfect." How do we know what perfect looks like? Today let's take time to learn the character of God our Father, so that we can begin to reflect Him.

Read Exodus 34:5–7 and write down the terms in which God spoke to describe Himself to Moses. I came up with seven. Did you find just as many? _____

_____

_____

_____ Let's look at these seven individually. Describe each in your own words.

Compassionate: _____
Psalm 86:15 says, "But you, O Lord, are a compassionate and gracious God, slow to anger, abounding in love and faithfulness." Compassion is a feeling of sympathy or sorrow for someone or something. In other words, someone with compassion feels pain for someone else that is in pain. God, your Father, suffers when you are in pain, and His heart breaks when He sees you cry.

**Gracious:** _____

Psalm 103:8 states, "The Lord is compassionate and gracious, slow to anger, abounding in love." (Sound familiar?) Grace means undeserved favor. So if someone is gracious, then he or she offers favor to the undeserving. You are undeserving of God's grace. Psalm 103:10 reminds us, "He does not treat us as our sins deserve or repay us according to our iniquities." He offers you grace that covers all your sins.

**Long-suffering:** _____

2 Peter 3:9 tells us, "The Lord is not slow in keeping His promise, as some understand slowness. He is patient ("long-suffering") with you, not wanting anyone to perish, but everyone to come to repentance." The Greek word for long-suffering is *"makrothymia"* and it means "forbearance; patience; disposition to endure long under offenses." How often is our God patient with us even after we offend Him?

**Love:** _____

1 John 4:16 tells us of God's love: "And so we know and rely on the love God has for us. God is love. Whoever lives in love lives in God, and God in him." God and love are interchangeable. They are the same. You cannot have love without God, nor can you have God without love.

**Faithfulness:** _____

Psalm 119:89–90 confirms that God's word is true, and He will remain faithful. "Your word, O Lord, is eternal; it stands firm in the heavens. Your faithfulness continues through all generations; you established the earth and it endures." Read Joshua 21:45: "Not one of all the Lord's good promises to the house of Israel failed; every one was fulfilled." How does it make you feel? He will keep His promises, and His word is the truth.

**Forgiving:** _____

God's goodness is shown through His forgiving nature. Psalm 107:8 declares that all men should praise the Lord "for His goodness and wonderful works to the children of men." Romans 2:4 teaches us not to ignore the goodness of God. "Or do you despise the riches of His goodness, forbearance, and longsuffering, not knowing that the goodness of God leads you to repentance?" His goodness is there to give you time to repent so that He can offer you His forgiveness.

**Just:** _____

God will give punishment where it is needed. He will not allow sin to continue without discipline and consequences. Romans 2:2 says, "Now we know that God's judgment against those who do such things is based on truth." He is a just God offering grace and mercy to those who will receive them, but He also judges those who will not turn from their wicked ways and repent.

Spend some time meditating on the character of God. Is your character reflective of His? Are these same seven traits evident in your own life? If not, ask Him to help you begin to mimic His character today. _____

_____

_____

_____

_____

_____

_____

_____

# What Is My Character?
## Day Two

Yesterday we discovered the personality of God our Father. We have no image or a physical representation to depict God, but we do have the example of His Son, Jesus.

"Character" translates in the Greek language as *"charakter,"* which means "the exact expression (the image) of any person or thing, marked likeness, precise reproduction in every respect." This word is used when describing Jesus Christ in Hebrews 1:3. Copy the first sentence of this verse here. _____

_____

_____

Some of your Bibles may say "express image" while others interpret as "exact representation." Who is it saying that the Son is the exact representation of? _____ Write in your own words what this verse is saying about Jesus. _____

_____

_____

Read John 14:9–11 and rewrite it in your own words. _____

_____

_____

Stay with me for a minute here. According to our last two Scriptures, Jesus is an exact representation of God, right? We just looked up Hebrews 1:3 and found out that Jesus was an exact image of our heavenly Father. So if this means that our *"charakter"* should be an expressed image of God the Father, the only visual representation of that is the life of Jesus Christ. He has the same character of His Father. Find the identical character trait for Jesus as we found yesterday for God in these following verses:

Hebrews 2:17 _____

Mark 6:34 _____

John 13:1 _____

Luke 23:34 _____

John 5:30 _____

John 1:14 _____

1 Timothy 1:16 _____

Jesus also walked on earth, His life given as a living example to us. He came to teach us, to show us the way. Copy John 14:6. _____

_____

_____

How do you get to the Father? _____

Read Matthew 11:29 and journal a quality of Jesus that you found. _____
Matthew 18:4 says, "Whosoever therefore shall humble himself as this little child, the same is greatest in the kingdom of heaven." Describe in your own words what it means to be humble. _____
_____Look up 1 Peter 5:5 and write down the word that means the opposite of humble. _____

In Philippians 2:7, what is the description given of Jesus? _____ What does the Bible say in Matthew 20:28 that Jesus came to do? _____
These last two traits partner with each other. You cannot be a true servant without having a humble spirit; neither can you be humble without first learning how to serve. Jesus did both.

What character trait is Jesus portraying when He says "may your will be done" in Matthew 26:42? _____ He tells us in John 14:31 "but the world must learn that I love the Father and that I do exactly what my Father has commanded me." Write what Jesus tells His Father in John 17:4. _____

_____

_____Jesus did not offer partial obedience. John 14:31 uses the word "exactly" and in John 17:4 He says he completed or finished the work of the Father. Obedience is not total submission unless it is done exactly and until completion.

As we strive to live like Jesus, learning His character, His example points us to God, our Lord and Savior. I can sum up our teaching over the past two days and encourage you today as Paul did to Timothy in 1 Timothy 6:11: "pursue righteousness, godliness, faith, love, endurance and gentleness."

Take a moment to be honest with yourself. Are there areas of your character that are not the "exact representation" of the life of Jesus? Talk to God about revealing those areas to you now. Ask Him to help you be an example to others just as He has been an example to you. _____

_____

_____

_____

_____

_____

_____

_____

# What Is My Character?
## Day Three

We have taken time to discover the character of God and of His Son Jesus so that we can reflect who they are through our own lives. But we realize the difficulties of living a perfect life as Jesus commanded in Matthew 5:48. God the Father made provision for us humans knowing that, alone, our flesh would never reach this pinnacle. Jesus explains God's plan in John 16:7–8. Who did He say God would send as our helper? _____
Write in your own words what Jesus says the Spirit will do in John 16:13–15. _____
_____
_____

Paul's prayer to the Ephesians in 3:16 is this: "I pray that out of His glorious riches He may strengthen you with power through His Spirit in your inner being." The Holy Spirit was sent to counsel the believer and to help empower him or her to live the Christian life (John 14:16). Paul gives us very specific instructions in the book of Galatians that we are to be led by the Holy Spirit (5:16). The Holy Spirit shares the same character and attributes with those of God the Father and God the Son. But, just like the other two members that complete the Trinity, the Holy Spirit also has specific character traits.

Copy John 15:5. _____
_____
_____ One of the tasks of the Holy Spirit is to counsel us to demonstrate the character of Jesus. Jesus teaches that if we abide in Him and He in us, we will bring forth much fruit. His desire is for us to produce good fruit. Read Matthew 7:17–19 and rewrite it in your own words. _____
_____
_____

Once again, as Paul is speaking in Galatians 5:22, he gives the church a list of attributes he calls the "fruits of the Spirit." So according to our above verses, what does this name mean to you? _____
_____

Jesus uses the example of the vine and fruit to illustrate the importance of being connected to Him. Our relationship to Him is the source of our spiritual growth. Our spiritual growth is made evident through the fruit we bear, or in other words the fruits of the Spirit. Read Galatians 5:22 and list the character of the Spirit. _____

_____

_____

Are any of these aspects new to what we have already discussed in the last few days? If so, which ones? _____

Two weeks ago, we spent some time discussing self-control, self-discipline, or temperance. So we won't cover it again, but let's do take a minute to talk about two additional traits of joy and peace.

The Bible says in Romans 14:17–18, "For the kingdom of God is not a matter of eating and drinking, but of righteousness, peace and joy in the Holy Spirit. Because anyone who serves Christ in this way is pleasing to God and approved by men." As the world searches in different places for happiness, Jesus tells us that joy is found only through the Holy Spirit. "If you obey my commandments, you will remain in my love; just as I have obeyed my Father's commandments, and remained in His love. I have told you this so that my joy may be in you, and that your joy may be complete" (John 15:10–11).

Just like many words in the English language, peace can have several different meanings. It could mean that two nations are not at war, or that there is harmony between two different people or groups. Read John 16:33. According to this verse, what does the word "peace" mean to you? _____ When I read this Scripture, I think of the phrase we often use: "peace of mind." In my own words, it's the absence of mental anxiety. Our peace can only come through Jesus. Read John 14:27. As Jesus gives us His peace, He warns us that it is different from the peace of the world. How do you think they differ? _____

_____

_____

_____

According to Romans 8:6, death comes when your mind is on the world, but life and peace are yours if your mind is controlled by the Spirit.

To live in your purpose as God intended for you when He created you, you must duplicate the character of God. Jesus came to earth and was a living testimony to us through His life, showing us how to imitate the nature of God. When He returned to heaven, the Father sent His Spirit to dwell within us to help us display His glory. Luke 6:44 says that every tree will be known by the fruit that it produces. What kind of fruit are you producing?

What do you feel the Spirit is speaking to you now? Journal your prayer to Him. _____

_____

_____

_____

_____

_____

_____

_____

# What Is My Character?
## Day Four

We have established that God's design was for us to be a reflection of Him and we do that with the help of the Spirit. Listen to what Paul says in 2 Corinthians 3:18: "And we, who with unveiled faces all reflect the Lord's glory, are being transformed into his likeness with ever-increasing glory, which comes from the Lord, who is the Spirit." As we begin to reflect the glory of God, we will be transformed. But there is no transformation like the change that comes from the Holy Spirit as He changes us from the inside, starting with our heart. He will begin the transformation within our character.

Read 1 John 2:4–6 and record how we know when someone truly knows God. _____
_____

As we begin to take on the character of Jesus, others will recognize Him within us. Read Acts 4:13. The elders and rulers had a realization. Who does it say that Peter and John had been with? _____ Jesus wants us to act like Him. Others will recognize our commitment by the fruit we bear.

As we begin to perfect our character, it is most important that we realize that God knows our reputation, including strengths and weaknesses. Look at Numbers 27:18 and write how God described Joshua. _____
_____ God knew Joshua's character and described him as one who has submitted himself to the spirit. This is who He wanted to be the next leader of the people of Israel. When your character reflects God, not only will others notice, but God himself is taking note. What is He saying about your character?

God's timing depends on our ability to be prepared. His concern is our heart and whether our character can prove strong when He needs us. Look up 1 Samuel 16:7 and record how God chooses the next leader for his people. _____
_____

We have already discussed back in week three that God will test us to help us grow. God tests us in order to strengthen our faith, question our commitment, examine our hearts, or check our ability to trust Him—all of which build character and lead us a little closer to being more like Him. Read Romans 5:3–4. What does this passage say that testing produces? _____ and _____ produces _____ and _____ produces _____.

Scan 2 Chronicles 32:31 and determine why God tested Hezekiah. _____

_____.

Turn to James 1:2–4. Write in your own words why we should rejoice in the suffering that comes from the test of God. _____

_____

In Job 1:2–3, the Scripture gives an account of the greatness of Job. "He had seven sons and three daughters, and he owned seven thousand sheep, three thousand camels, five hundred yoke of oxen and five hundred donkeys, and had a large number of servants. He was the greatest man among all the people of the East." But when Satan came in front of God and God gave an account of Job, none of these things mattered. Write how God narrated Job's reputation. (v. 8) _____

_____ God offered Job to Satan. He initiated the conversation and the testing of Job. God knew Job's character. He was confident that Job would pass the test and when he did, God rewarded him double for his faithfulness (Job 42:10–17). If Satan and God were having a dialog in heaven, would God offer you as one that was upright and blameless? Could He be confident that if he allowed Satan to have his way with you that you would remain faithful to Him?

To review, others recognize our commitment by the _____ we bear. God is taking note of our _____. God will test our character to help us _____. Remember 1 Corinthians 10:13: "No temptation has seized you except what is common to man. And God is faithful; He will not let you be tempted beyond what you can bear. But when you are tempted, He will also provide a way out so that you can stand up under it."

Thank God for the testing and the building of your character. Ask Him to teach you how to focus more on your inward qualities and less on your outward appearance. What is He saying to you now about your character? Talk to Him about your inadequacies. _____

_____

_____

_____

*Molly Hardin*

_____

_____

_____

_____

_____

# What Is My Character?
## Day Five

We have spent the majority of this week discovering what it looks like to have a godly character. I have realized over the years that the clarity of right and wrong has been blurred. What I mean by that is that things that were once considered ungodly have been compromised and are not rejected so quickly by Christians. I want to spend this day giving clarity to what God considers sin.

In Galatians 5, just as Paul gave a list of the characteristics of the Spirit, he also gave warning to the church of a sinful nature. Copy his list in verses 19–21. _____

_____

_____ Let's take a few minutes to dissect some of these sins. Let me note that some translations add and others omit adultery. Regardless if your Bible includes this act in your list or not, it would certainly be covered under the next definition of "sexual immorality" or "fornication." I will address them together.

Sexual immorality (whether married or not, this addresses all sexual sins): *Webster's Dictionary* defines fornication as "Voluntary sexual intercourse between two unmarried persons or two persons not married to each other."[7] So this covers sex before and outside marriage. There may be some people who have been deceived by the definition of marriage. I won't go into great detail—look up the definition and study the concept. However, in Genesis 2:24, the Bible is clear that marriage consists of one male and one female, and they will abandon everything for each other and they will become united together as one, as equals. Sexual immorality can be defined as all premarital sexual acts. Just so there is no room for miscommunication, if you are participating in an activity that would cause your mind to take your body to places it should not yet go, you have crossed the line.

Impurity: The original word in the King James Version is "uncleanness." This is a broad word that can cover a multitude of sins. Impurity is the opposite of purity; if it isn't pure, it is impure. This covers your speech, including jokes and insinuations. Impurity covers the misconception and justification of standing on the boundary line but not crossing over. It covers the argument of putting yourself in a compromising situation. Impure is anything that is not clean.

Debauchery means "excessive indulgence or self-indulgence." The original King James Version used the word "lewdness." This means "obscene, vulgar, or a total disregard to restraint as far as sexual behavior is concerned." With lewd behavior, one has no shame and will flaunt his or her immorality publicly.

Idolatry is the worship of anything above God our Father. This includes worship of an altered God from what is revealed as truth and a God that has been conformed to the opinions of man. This also includes the idea that God is something or allows some things that are contrary to His word. The most common idolatry that is practiced today is the politically correct God. There is one true living God; anything that is placed before Him is considered idolatry.

Witchcraft is the worship of supernatural powers and evil spirits. An additional definition is the practice, art, or spells of a person who tries to influence fate or fortune. This word translates in the Greek as "*pharmakeia*," where we get our word *pharmacy*. The meaning is the use or the administering of drugs; poisoning. In biblical times, as well as today, many people took drugs to hallucinate or to alter their views of life. Both reasons are seen as sin in the eyes of God. We were created to glorify God. At any time if we are glorifying anything other than God, we are bringing glory to Satan and his works. Therefore, we would be practicing witchcraft.

Hatred is the condition of our attitude as we treat others. It is a sin of the attitude of the heart and is in direct conflict with the greatest commandment given in Mark 12:30–31: "Love your neighbor as yourself."

Discord is translated as "contention and strife." Discord means "controversy, disputes, conflict, and disagreement." It is even defined as "competition." Have you been stubborn and refused to change your ways and commented that it is just a friendly competition? Maybe you need to check your motives. It is okay to not always agree with everyone and everything. However, to stay in that disagreement, creating conflict and strife, is sin in the eyes of God.

Jealousy is the desire to have what someone else has or be what someone else is. If you wish that things were different for you and they were like someone else's situation, you are guilty of jealousy. If you can think of someone that you would consider an active "rival" to you, question your heart and look for areas of jealousy. 1 Timothy 6:6–9 says, "But godliness with contentment is great gain. For we brought nothing into the world, and we can take nothing out of it. But if we have food and clothing, we will be content with that. People who want to get rich fall into temptation and a trap and into many foolish and harmful desires that plunge men into ruin and destruction."

"Fits of rage" means to lose your temper or lose your self-control. Usually this person cannot control his or her anger once the outburst happens. There are no discrepancies between "Something just set me off" and "I took it as long as I could and just got pushed overboard." God called us to a life of long-suffering self-control and to demonstrate the love of God.

Selfish ambition is a motivation for personal gain and its only aim is for profit and power. It means to be self-seeking and to always be looking out for one's own interest regardless of the welfare of others. Jesus taught us the opposite—to surrender ourselves for the needs of others and to be motivated for the interest of God alone.

Dissension means "a division or break in unity." Sometimes our talk and gossip can cause dissension between two friends. Dissension is also defined as a disagreement. Most often we use it as a two-step process. When a disagreement has happened, we will talk about it until we have affected everyone with dissension within our group. Negative talk can break the unity within a church, work place, or family and friends.

Faction: The original word used in the King James Bible is "heresies." This word is a stronger emphasis on the word dissension. The best way to understand is that it is the wrongful splitting over a difference of opinions. This is the foundation of most church denominations today. Many split because of an irreconcilable difference of opinions. A better way to define faction would be to refuse to change your opinion because you are right and everyone else is wrong.

Envy: This word has a meaning close to the meaning of jealousy and sometimes we use the two words interchangeably. But envy doesn't mean so much that you want what someone else has, but you are resentful at them for having it. This doesn't have to be material things. It could be another's success, appearance, family, or, worse, his or her spiritual gifting or ministry from God.

Drunkenness: While this may seem obvious, I want to define the term so there is no room for doubt. This word does not necessarily mean "can't walk around" drunk. Of course, this passage will include that level of drinking, but this word translates as "intoxicated." Intoxicated can be described as being impaired in any way by the consumption of alcohol. Whether you are a Christian that believes it is okay to drink or not to drink, this passage leaves no room for argument. If your mind or body is impaired by an alcoholic beverage, it is sin.

Orgies: The original word used in the King James is "revelries." This means an unrestrained party or a boisterous festivity. These parties consist of heavy drinking, sexual activity, and the indulgence of fleshly desires.

I know today's study was long, but I felt like it was very important that you have a clear understanding of what God says is opposite of His nature and His character.

I will end on a positive note and continue to read the remainder of this chapter and remind you what it means to be led by the Spirit. Galatians 5:21b–26 says, "I warn you, as I did before, that those who live like this will not inherit the kingdom of God. But the fruit of the Spirit is love, joy, peace, patience, kindness, goodness, faithfulness, gentleness and self-control. Against such things, there is no law. Those who belong to Christ Jesus have crucified the sinful nature with its passions and desires. Since we live by the Spirit, let us keep in step with the Spirit. Let us not become conceited, provoking and envying each other."

Pray that God will strengthen you to keep in step with the Spirit as He helps you to continue to crucify the sinful nature and its passions and desires. Ask Him to reveal any area in your life that does not line up with His character. Pray that He will instruct you on how to become righteous and blameless in His sight. _____

_____

_____

_____

_____

_____

_____

_____

# Week Seven

## Character Makes Trust Possible
## Day One

Last week we looked at the importance of having a godly character. We discovered what qualities are reflective of God our Father and what He requires from us as we demonstrate them. This week we are going to talk about why these habits are important.

Your character is a blend of your morals and behaviors that make you who you are. Other people will define you by your character. For example, some might say, "I'm not going to tell her; she tells everything she knows," or "I'm not going to ask him to do it; it will take him three weeks to get it done and then it still won't be done right." On a positive note, one could say, "She's a great student. She's hardworking and such a pleasure to have in class." How do others describe you? Look up Daniel 6:4 and write down how his character was described. _____

_____Men were watching Daniel and were trying to catch him making a mistake but could find no fault in him.

People who know you know your character. It's who you are, how you live, and what you do. What they know about your reputation determines whether or not they trust you. Reflect on this statement by John Maxwell: "Character makes trust possible. And trust makes leadership possible."[8] Let's take a minute to break this statement down a bit.

If I say I trust you, it means that I have confidence in you. It could mean that I trust that you are going to do what you say, or that I have confidence that I am safe or my possessions are safe with you. I also may allow my children to go somewhere without me because I trust that they will make the right decisions in my absence. Past experiences between two people either build or destroy trust. Your character communicates whether or not you are a trustworthy person. If others cannot trust you, then you simply cannot lead them. Trust is the foundation of your ability to lead. People want a leader who is dependable, honest, faithful, and constant.

In the book of Exodus, Moses receives some very good advice from his father-in-law. He alone had been handling disputes and answering questions for the people of Israel. After Jethro saw what was happening, he advised Moses to appoint several leaders over the tribes to serve as judges for the people. Read Exodus 18:21 and list the character traits of the leaders that Jethro recommended he choose. _____ _____ Why do you think these particular qualities are important? _____ _____

Look up Proverbs 25:13. What do you think is meant by "coolness of snow at harvest time"? _____ _____ Imagine working in the garden when the crops are ready to be harvested. Can you picture how hot you might become? Think of how it might feel if someone brings you a glass of water that was cooled by melting snow. It would "refresh your spirit." This is the same idea in this proverb. A trustworthy servant brings peace and joy to his master. Write down what Jesus said about being trustworthy in Matthew 5:37. _____ _____ _____

Joshua established a relationship of trust with the people of Israel long before it was his time to lead. With the death of Moses, the fear of the unknown was a heavy burden to carry. The people could have questioned God. They might have asked why He would bring them all the way to the property line and after forty years leave them without a leader. But instead of a time of instability, they followed Joshua with a determination and unwavering love. Look at Joshua 1:16–17. What was the response of the people? _____ _____ _____

It is important to know that trust is earned and it comes with a lifetime of experiences. Each positive experience moves one a little closer to full abandonment of doubt and total belief in the other person. You must establish a godly character of integrity and honor with those that God has entrusted you to lead. Your ability to lead lies in the ability of your followers to trust in you, and only your unblemished character makes trust possible.

Are you trustworthy? Can others have confidence in you? Does your *yes* mean *yes* and your *no* mean *no?* Ask the Holy Spirit to show you areas in your life that need some work. Ask God to help you become a man or woman of integrity and build a character of trustworthiness. _____

_____

_____

_____

_____

_____

# Character Makes Trust Possible
## Day Two

Your character is constantly on display in public, but its development begins in private. I found a saying years ago from an anonymous source that sounds like this: "Be careful of your thoughts, for your thoughts become your words. Be careful of your words, for your words become your actions. Be careful of your actions, for your actions become your habits. Be careful of your habits, for your habits become your character. Be careful of your character, for your character becomes your destiny." Meditate on this for a few minutes.

Your character is developing through a process that begins with your thoughts. Your thoughts are private. No one can hear or see them. You might think that you can keep hiding them in private while living something different in public, but eventually they will be exposed through your character.

What do you think about when no one is around? Write down the stages of sin listed in James 1:14–15.

1. _____

2. _____

3. _____

Read Psalm 94:11 and record who knows what you are thinking. _____
_____ How pleased is God with your thoughts? Record Proverbs 15:26. _____
_____
_____According to our Scripture, God knows your thoughts and He detests those that are wicked but is pleased with those that are pure. Read 1 Chronicles 28:9 and write down what God will do with every thought. _____
_____
_____
_____

Is it true that sometimes your thoughts just come and go and they do their own thing? You don't necessarily choose to think ungodly thoughts; it just happens. Impure thoughts are not sin, but when we begin to entertain those thoughts, acting as if they are harmless, then they become sin. You must stand guard over your mind. You must be disciplined in your thought process. Look up these next few verses and note what we are to do to keep our thoughts pleasing to God.

Hebrews 3:1 _____

Romans 13:14 _____

Philippians 4:8 _____

When sinful thoughts enter your mind, you must be proactive and consciously change those thoughts to focus on things that are pure and godly. Once you create a habit in cleaning up your thoughts, it will begin to be revealed in your words, actions, habits, character, and finally your destiny. How does Jesus explain this process in Matthew 23:26?

_____

_____

Satan knows how powerful the mind is. He knows how to play those mind games. He wants to deceive you and to keep you from learning the truth. Remember when we read of Satan and Eve in the garden (Genesis 3:1–7). Satan asked Eve a question: "Did God *really* say …?" She answered his question and then Satan got her in a place where she began to reason and ponder in her own mind until she convinced herself to believe something that was not true. Then he said to her, "*Surely* you will not die." Satan will quietly put thoughts into your mind. You have to make the decision of whether you will ponder these thoughts. We learned earlier that pondering leads to actions and the actions of sin lead to death. In Luke 10:19, Jesus says that he has given you the authority to overcome the powers of the enemy and this includes the thoughts he puts in your mind. In 2 Corinthians 10:5, Paul tells the church to "take captive every thought and make it obedient to Christ." By following this command, we learn to be disciplined and to take authority over each scheme of the enemy to plant seeds of sin in our minds.

Have you allowed yourself to entertain impure thoughts? How can you protect your mind from these thoughts in the future? _____

_____ Write a prayer

asking God to forgive you and to help you become disciplined in your mind. Ask Him to help you replace evil thoughts for those about Him. _____

_____

_____

_____

_____

_____

_____

# Character Makes Trust Possible
## Day Three

Have you ever followed a leader and eventually lost your trust in him? Think about that time. What happened to cause your attitude toward him to change? As we talked about earlier, trust is earned and it comes after many experiences. Sometimes those experiences cause us to build a foundation of trust, but other times trust is lost through the mistakes we may make.

You will mess up and will begin to lose confidence of others. However, what you do after your mistake is vital to your leadership future. Hear this profound statement made by PepsiCo chairman and CEO Craig Weatherup: "People will tolerate honest mistakes, but if you violate their trust you will find it very difficult to ever regain their confidence."[9]

You will make mistakes, and people will be watching. But people also know that you are human and are willing to forgive as long as you admit your mistake, accept responsibility for those mistakes and learn from them, and keep from repeating your mistake. Tomorrow we are going to talk about honest mistakes, but today let's look at a leader's betrayal. What do you think is meant by the second half of Mr. Weatherup's comment? In your own words, what does it mean to violate someone's trust? _____ _____ If you abuse, intentionally disrespect, or do not cherish the trust someone has given you, then you will lose it. It is a very difficult process to regain this trust, therefore hindering your ability to continue to lead this person.

One of the greatest biblical stories on betrayal is found in Genesis 29. Read verses 15-30 but write down what Jacob says to Laban in verse 25. _____ _____How would you have felt if you were Jacob? _____ _____ Would it have been hard for you to trust Laban and work an additional seven years? _____ Read Genesis 29:10 and write how Jacob and Laban were related. _____ Does it surprise you that this betrayal was from a relative? _____ Why or why not? _____ _____

We already know that Laban deceived Jacob, but did we forget that this dad conned his daughters too? Laban switched his daughters at the last minute and caused a lifetime of competition and hatred between these two sisters. Read Genesis 30:15. Do you think there is some resentment between Leah and Rachel? _____ Their father's deceit created years of jealousy. Too many times the family members we trust and rely on will betray us.

Just like in Laban's case, sometimes leaders will intentionally lie and deceive others to benefit themselves. Sometimes it is to move ahead in life and be described as successful. Other times it can be to prosper financially or gain something from somebody else. Either way, God's purpose for you was to lead others to Him. You do this by gaining their trust. If you intentionally violate their trust to elevate yourself, you will pay the price.

God used the deception of Laban to develop Jacob's character. As we started this study today, we began the story of Jacob as he was on the run from his family and looking for his kin. We have to back up a few chapters to find out what had happened. Read Genesis 27:1–36. What did Jacob do to Esau? _____ _____

Read Genesis 27:18–29. Who did Jacob deceive in these verses? _____ _____ Look at Genesis 27:35 and tell how Isaac describes what Jacob did. _____ Are you feeling like Jacob got what he deserved? _____

God had a plan to do great things through Jacob, but because his character would not permit him to gain trust of others, God allowed a time of trials to reshape it. Isaac was a wealthy man, so Jacob was not necessarily used to hard work. The servants did the work for his dad. But now for twenty years Jacob became a servant of Laban. This was an essential tool to developing his character.

Laban took advantage of Jacob and his love for Rachel. He knew he could get Jacob to stay and work as his servant seven more years for Rachel, so he switched daughters after the long ceremony and in the dark of the night. Leah enters the dark tent wearing a veil. Once the morning light came up, Jacob discovered the trade.

God used this time to humble Jacob and to shape his character to be more pleasing to God. Jacob left Laban to reconcile with his brother whom he had deceived twenty years earlier.

He came to him humiliated and bowing down, calling himself his humble servant. His character changed only after he had his own experience with deception and greed.

Have you violated someone's trust? Honestly, can you admit when you make a mistake? Becoming a humble servant of the people you lead is the only way you will be able to gain their trust. Talk to God today about what the Holy Spirit is revealing to you about your character. _____

_____

_____

_____

_____

_____

_____

_____

# Character Makes Trust Possible
## Day Four

You are human and you will make mistakes. Even great leaders make mistakes. How you handle these mistakes is crucial to your future as a leader. As a mistake is just coming into light, a leader has been given an opportunity. Leaders are separated from imposters depending upon how they will handle that opportune moment.

People will tolerate your honest mistakes, but you have to let them know that it was an honest mistake. As a leader, you are standing at a crossroads. You can either deny the mistake, blame it on another, completely ignore it and act like it was intentional, or you can admit that you are human, accept responsibility for your actions and move forward with determination and credibility.

Many leaders try to cover up and hide their mistakes. Read 1 Samuel 15:19–31. What leadership mistakes do you see that Saul is making in this last conversation between him and Samuel? _____

_____

Saul first lied about his mission, secondly he blamed his sin on the people, and finally he asked Samuel to cover his sins and hide them from the people.

Read Joshua 9:1–27. What does it say that Joshua did not do in verse 14? _____

_____

There is no doubt that the Gibeonites planned and preconceived deception to trick Joshua and some of the leaders into making a treaty with them instead of killing them and taking their land. Look up these following three verses and write down what God tells the Children of Israel not to do.

1.  Exodus 34:12 _____

2.  Deuteronomy 7:2 _____

3.  Deuteronomy 23:6 _____

What does Joshua do in Joshua 9:15? _____

Can you see where there is a problem? God was really clear on what to do if someone wanted to make a treaty. Joshua disobeyed Him.

In 9:16–17 Joshua and the leaders realized that they had been deceived. Joshua confessed that he had been conned (Joshua 9:16–22) but continued to keep his word. After the people grumbled and were mad at the leaders, the acted honorably by keeping their oath, even if it was an oath made out of deception. These leaders had integrity and proved they could be trusted by keeping their word. Joshua proved that as a human he may make mistakes, but he could be trusted.

The Bible tells us in Romans that we all have fallen short and we all have sinned. That's who we are; we are flesh made from the dust of the ground and are nothing without Jesus Christ. Your mistakes do not have to destroy your leadership you have worked so hard to achieve. Look up Proverbs 28:13 and rewrite it in your own words. _____

_____

_____

The mistake many leaders make is trying to cover, hide, and cast blame on others for their sins. Don't fall into this trap. Some care more about their image than their character. They care more about what others think about them than they care what God thinks. The first example of this behavior was demonstrated in the Garden of Eden. Look up Genesis 3:12–14 and take note of Adam and Eve's ability to blame others. What excuse did Adam give for eating the fruit? _____

_____

_____

What excuse did Eve give for eating the fruit? _____

_____

_____

Neither Adam nor Eve could admit to God that they were really to blame for the sin that they had committed. They couldn't accept the responsibility and ask for forgiveness. Instead, they pointed fingers at someone else to cover their own weaknesses. Turn to 2 Corinthians 12:9 and copy it down below. _____

_____

_____ Unless we admit our weaknesses, God's power will never be able to be made known through us.

People will begin to lose faith in you as a leader if you continue to serve your own interest. It will only take a short time in the life of a leader for his true heart and character to be revealed. People will follow your character before they follow your words. In other words, do you practice what you preach? Do you walk the walk or just talk the talk? And when you do fail and make a mistake, how do you handle that mistake?

Joshua made a mistake by giving his word and made a treaty with the Gibeonites. But once he made a covenant, he not only kept his oath to allow them to live, but he even came to their rescue when they needed it. Read Joshua 10:6–8. Joshua's integrity went a step past just keeping his word; he went into battle to defend those that deceived him. How far will you go and what price will you pay to gain the trust of the people you will lead?

Ask God to help you conquer pride and the self-centeredness that sometimes wars in the minds of leaders. _____

_____

_____

_____

_____

_____

_____

_____

# Character Makes Trust Possible
## Day Five

Ethics is a word with lost meaning in our society today. Failed leaders are not just politicians, CEOs, and businessmen. Corruption is rampant in our churches, homes, and neighborhoods. We rarely stop to acknowledge another scandalous story that flashes on the television screen. It is accepted. It is a way of life these days. But because of this lifestyle, people are finding it very hard to completely trust someone who is in a leadership position.

The most important job of any leader is to first build trust. We have talked over the past week that trust is built by your character. You must first build credibility with your followers. Credibility means that you are believable. People can trust what you say. Let's go back to study Joshua and take note of his practices that created credibility, which in turn created trust from the people so that when it was his time to lead, they would follow.

Why Joshua? What did he have that the others didn't? How did he build trust when the others couldn't? What was his character?

First of all, Joshua was available to be used by God. He was willing to go when God said, "Go." Read Numbers 27:15–23. Joshua could have argued with God just as Moses did when he was appointed leader in Exodus chapters 3 and 4. But Joshua accepted his assignment and made a choice to lead. Read Joshua 1:1–10 and copy down verse 10. _____

_____

_____ It was a simple acceptance: "So Joshua ordered."

Joshua had the heart of a servant. How is Joshua described in Exodus 24:13 and 33:11? __
_____ He served the man of God for over forty years. As he served, he learned. Joshua had a teachable spirit. Read the story of a teaching moment in Joshua's life found in Numbers 11:26–30. What do you think was the lesson learned in this Scripture? _____

_____

_____

Back up and read 11:16–17. Why did Moses gather the leaders? _____
_____

The children of Israel needed more leadership and God was taking some burden off Moses. In verse 25, God took the same spirit that was on Moses and put that spirit on these leaders. They needed the same vision, and they needed to be in unity. In verse 26, why do you think these two men did not go to the Tent of Meeting? _____
Joshua apparently felt that they were being defiant and might undermine Moses' ministry. Would you have felt the same way? _____ Why or why not? _____
_____

How did Moses respond? _____
_____ He certainly didn't sound worried. His desire was for everyone to have the Lord's spirit. For if they had the same spirit, they would all be following God's heart.

Additionally, Joshua knew that alone he could do nothing, but with God he could do everything. Look up Numbers 14:6–9 and write down why he told the people they could defeat the enemy and take the land. _____
_____He believed God and trusted in His words. Joshua trusted God because he loved Him. How does Numbers 32:12 describe how Joshua followed God? _____

Joshua was obedient from the first time we met him in Exodus 17 until his death in Joshua 24. Rewrite again Joshua 11:15, the testimony of Joshua's obedience to man and God. ____
_____

Throughout this entire manual, we have discovered ways that you can develop the skills necessary to become a great leader of God. But there are some things that you can't do and they must be left up to God and His perfect plan and timing.

Read Deuteronomy 1:37–38. Joshua was chosen by God. John 15:19 says, "If you belonged to the world, it would love you as its own. As it is, you do not belong to the world, but I have chosen you out of the world." You have been chosen by God to lead.

Read Deuteronomy 3:28. Joshua was called by God. You have a purpose and were created to fulfill that purpose. God has a calling for your life. The time will come and you will receive that call. Will you be ready when it comes?

Deuteronomy 31:14 tells us that there came a time that God commissioned Joshua to take the lead. His character was being developed over the years so that when the time came to be commissioned he would be ready.

Most importantly, the people listened and followed Joshua. Copy Deuteronomy 34:9 and write down why the people followed him. _____

_____

The most important quality you can have as a godly leader is to be filled with the Spirit, God's spirit of wisdom.

Take a minute to meditate on today's lesson. Journal what you need to say to God now.

_____

_____

_____

_____

_____

_____

_____

_____

# Week Eight

## If and Then
## Day One

As we bring the previous seven weeks to a close, I want to take these next few days to teach you a lesson that will go with you for a lifetime. Not only is this a prerequisite to becoming a great leader, but it is mandatory to becoming a great man or woman of God. These next few pages hold the key to living an abundant life in Jesus Christ. I want to teach you the way of God. He offers us our heart's desires and all that we need to be satisfied in Him. He also shares the keys to being successful and having a prosperous life.

God is a God of love and promise. Because of His love, He is also a God that offers freedom of choices. He loves you so much that He will never force Himself on you. God is a conditional God. The word condition means that an agreement was made on certain terms. Now this may surprise you and it may not feel right to you for me to tell you that many of God's promises come with certain conditions. I will spend more time on this as the week continues, but first I want to show you some promises from God that require nothing from you in return.

Turn in your Bible to Hebrews 13:5 and copy the promise from God. _____
_____
_____

He promises to be with you wherever you go and through whatever you may face. His promise is that you will never be alone; you will never be without Him.

He also promises to love you unconditionally. He loved you so much that He sent His Son, who came and laid down His life voluntarily take your punishment for sin. And even after all of this, He said that there is nothing that you will ever be able to do to make Him stop loving you. He will love you no matter what you do to Him in return. Look up Romans 8:35–39 and rewrite His promise to you in your own words. _____
_____

_____ Read Psalm 136 and note how many times His word communicates that God's love endures forever. Circumstances will come and go, the world will change and people will fail you, but His love for you endures forever. And forever, my friend, is a very long time.

God promises His children that they will never be in need of anything. Copy the promise found in Philippians 4:19. _____

_____

_____ In 2 Corinthians 12:9, He promises that His grace is sufficient for us and, whatever we may be going through, He is all we need. "My grace is sufficient for you, for My power is made perfect in weakness." God told Paul in this case, instead of taking away the pain of his burden, He would give him His grace, and His grace was all that Paul needed. In studying these two verses, we learn that God will either provide for your need according to His riches, or He will strengthen your character to allow you to be able to carry your load. Either way, He will provide what you need.

Copy what the Bible says about the integrity of God's words in Numbers 23:19. _____

_____

_____

_____ Do not judge God's word like you would judge the word of a human. He cannot lie and He will not change His mind. In this world of corruption and disappointments, many of you have been hurt by the word of man. Some of you find it very difficult to trust others because of past experiences. You can trust God and trust Him to keep His promises. Rewrite in your own words Joshua 21:45 and Joshua 23:14. _____

_____

_____

Isn't it great to know that we have the confidence of God's unfailing love? Because He loves us so much, He will never leave us alone without our needs being met. What He says, He will do, and you can trust in that. Regardless of what man may say or do, how he may deceive or disappoint, there is one in whom you can always depend to keep His word and that is Jesus Christ.

Ask Him today to help you trust totally in Him. If you have past hurts that keep you from trusting in Him, tell Him about those times today. His grace is sufficient for you. _____

_____

_____

_____

_____

_____

_____

_____

# If and Then
## Day Two

It would be unfair of me to spend this week teaching you about the promises of God and never teach you that He is a God that offers conditional promises. He offers you choices. He created you with a will, a will to choose and make decisions for yourself. Let's take a few minutes for me to explain this in everyday terms before we go trudging off into the Scripture.

You may hear someone say, "We'll go swimming this afternoon if it doesn't rain." By hearing this statement, you can assume that you will be going swimming as long as it doesn't start to rain. You can also assume that if it does start raining, you will not be going swimming.

Sometimes these statements are expressed using the conditional words "if" and "then." Look at the example above: "We'll go swimming this afternoon *if* it doesn't rain." This statement could have been said like this: "If it doesn't rain this afternoon, then we will go swimming." These two sentences mean the same thing, but I used the conditional words "if" and "then."

Let's look at times when decisions in our life are conditional but are not spoken. For instance, we all know that for a car to be used as transportation, we must keep gasoline in the tank. So the condition is "If I don't put gas in my car, then I will not be able to drive to my destination." What if this destination is my job? If I don't drive to work, then I could lose my job. I'll give you another example and you fill in the blank: I have a test tomorrow. If I don't study for the test, then _____. Finish this one: These are the rules at school. If I break one of these rules, then_____

_____

_____. Then my parents will _____

_____

_____

Some of God's promises are conditional promises. This means that we have to do something to receive something in return, just like in our examples above. If you put gas in your car, then you can drive it to your destination. If you don't put gas in, then there is no other way to make that car move on its own.

Let's look at Romans 10:9. Fill in the blanks: "If you _____ with your mouth, 'Jesus is Lord,' and _____ in your heart that God raised Him from the dead, *then* _____." Go to 10:13. What do you have to do to be saved? _____

_____ .

Don't misunderstand what I am telling you. Salvation is free and Jesus died so that you don't have to die. But salvation is a free *gift*. And each gift requires something from us. We must first receive that gift and open it before it becomes ours. Look at Romans 6:23. What is the payment for sin? _____ What is the gift of God? _____ We have to receive God's gift of life, but how? Look carefully at John 3:16. I know you know this verse, but look it up anyway and let's look for key words you may not have ever seen before. How do I accept His gift of eternal life? _____ _____ So I could write it this way. If I believe in Him, then I should not die but have eternal life. It works the other way as well. I cannot have eternal life unless I believe in Him. If I don't believe in Christ, then I cannot be saved (Romans 10:13).

Write the "if" and "then" condition found in 1 John 1:9. If we _____ _____*then* he is faithful and just to _____ _____and cleanse us from all unrighteousness.

God gives conditional promises in many areas of our lives—not just with the gift of salvation. Go back to a well-known verse in Proverbs 3:5–6 and write down His conditional promise. _____

_____

_____

_____ You must first put your trust in the Lord and in everything you do acknowledge Him, and then He will direct your paths. Fill in the blanks of these commonly spoken promises and take note of your responsibility for God to fulfill them.

1. John 14:14: "If you ask anything in my name, _____

_____ ."

2.  Matt. 6:33: "But seek ye first the kingdom of God and His righteousness and _____
    _____."

3.  Matt. 7:7: "Ask and _____, seek and _____,
    knock and _____."

God's conditional promises require faith from me. I must believe in Him. I must trust Him. I must seek Him, love Him, ask from Him, and believe that He will do what He said. It requires active initiation from me, giving up, and surrendering everything to allow Him to do what He wills for my life. Talk to Him now about having complete surrender for His will. Ask the Holy Spirit to show you if you have been keeping your end of the bargain to do what He asks of you. _____

_____

_____

_____

_____

_____

_____

_____

# If and Then
## Day Three

Just as we learned on the first day of this week, conditional terms can be used for either positive or negative promises. For example, we decided that if you put gasoline in your car, it could be used to take you where you need to go. But if you fail to add gas to your tank, then your car is useless in travel. It is a choice that you are given. You can choose to add gas, or you can choose to accept the consequences. The same is true with the promises of God. Let's look at God's first promise recorded in Genesis 2:17. Copy the verse here.

_____

_____

_____ Write in your own words the "if" and "then" condition that God gave Adam. _____

_____ So what was the choice that Adam and Eve could have made? To eat or not to eat, right?

Adam and Eve both knew of the consequences of eating the fruit. God told Adam in the above verse, but Eve also told Satan in Genesis 3:3. There is always a consequence to the choices that you will make. This was explained to you in elementary school as cause and effect. The effect is determined by the cause. In other words, if you do something it will make something else happen. Effect happens as the result of the cause. For example, you got grounded because you made a D on a test. The cause is the D and the effect is your punishment. You made a D on a test because you went out with friends and did not study for your test. The cause is that you did not study, and the D is the effect. We have choices to make every day, and with every choice there is a consequence or a cause.

Look at Deuteronomy 30:15. Moses is speaking to the children of Israel and explaining this very thing to them. "See, I set before you today life and prosperity, death and destruction." He explained to them that the choices they made in life would determine life or death, prosperity or destruction. Continue reading in 30:16–18 and write these promises in your own words. _____

_____

_____

I am going to ask you to take some time reading today. I think it is extremely important to hear the words of the Lord in the verses that I will give you. We will also build upon each of these chapters in the next two days. Read Deuteronomy 28:1–14. Read it all; don't get lazy at the end of our journey.

Go back and reread 28:1–2. Write the "if" and "then" promise given by the Lord our God.

_____

_____

_____

_____

Not only does God offer blessings and prosperity for obedience, but He also promises curses and pain for disobedience. Read Deuteronomy 28:15–68. Write the "if" and "then" promise given in 28:15. _____

_____Write the curse given in the middle of the verse of Deuteronomy 28:29. "You will be _____ in _____ you do." Look at 28:45 and write why you will be cursed. _____

God gave a formula for blessings as well as a path to curses. He gave you a choice with an "if" and "then." Your decision determines your consequences. You are the cause to the effect. Moses gives another warning in Deuteronomy 29:16–19. Write down these three things.

1. _____ (v. 18)

2. _____ (v. 18)

3. _____ (v. 19)

In Deuteronomy 29:29, Moses says, "The secret things belong to the Lord our God, but the things revealed belong to us and to our children forever, that we may follow all the words of this law." The secret things that Moses is talking about are the things for our lives that God keeps to himself. For example, He keeps secret our future, His plans sometimes, and other things that He will reveal in His timing.

However, "the things revealed belong to us and to our children …" He has revealed what He will do in terms of blessings for obedience and curses for disobedience. He has revealed the truth to you and you have the words of His commandments and His laws.

Read Deuteronomy 30:19–20 and meditate on the choices of life. What do you need to say to God now?

_____

_____

_____

_____

_____

_____

_____

_____

# If and Then
## Day Four

Now that I have laid the groundwork and you clearly understand that life is full of choices and God offers conditions, I want to show you the simplest answer to living the abundant life that God desires for you. God gave Joshua the key to the success of the Israelites in Joshua 1:7–8. What is the "if" and "then" condition given in these verses? _____
_____

The success of this great leader was conditional. God promised him success wherever he went (Joshua 1:7) and prosperity (v. 8). But it was not automatic. Joshua wasn't going to have all the success and prosperity without doing something in return. Many of us know this principle but are making this promise too hard. There is nothing that you can do in your own efforts to bring success to you. Success does not come to those with the most education, most money, or friends in high places. Success comes by obeying God's law and doing everything written in it.

So what is the law that Moses gave him? What do you think God means in Joshua 1:8 when He says, "Book of the Law"? _____
_____

The Book of the Law was the laws and instructions that God had given Moses to this point. Reading from Exodus 21:1, God says, "These are the laws you are to set before them." For the next ten or so chapters, God continues to declare the rules to Moses. Exodus 24:4 states, "Moses then wrote down everything the Lord had said." Exodus 34:27 states, "Then the Lord said to Moses, "Write down these words, for in accordance with these words I have made a covenant with you and with Israel." The Book of the Law would be the same to the Israelites as our Bible is to us.

In your opinion, what does God mean when He tells Joshua, "Do not let this Book of the Law depart from your mouth?" _____
_____ The first time
we hear this wording is in Exodus 4:15. God is telling Moses that He will allow Aaron to

speak for him. God tells Moses to put his words into Aaron's mouth. Write Exodus 4:16.

_____

_____ Moses will put his words in Aaron's mouth and God will tell both of them what to say. The goal is that you always want God's words in your mouth, so that the words that you are speaking are not your own but are His. You do not want to lose His words by neglecting them and therefore forgetting what He said. That is why God tells Joshua to meditate on them day and night. He wants him to do everything he can to keep His words close to his heart.

Before you get uptight about all the laws in the first five books of the Bible, let me give you some peace. Of course there were commandments that were given thousands of years ago that do not apply to us today. For example, we do not follow the law about sacrifices that were to be offered for sin. The death and resurrection of Jesus Christ removed the need to offer payment for our sins. He became the living sacrifice and paid for all sins past, present, and future. Also, rules have changed in regard to punishment for sins and restitution for wrong. In other words, today we certainly could not stone Achan and his entire family along with his cattle, donkeys, and sheep as punishment for his disobedience (Joshua 7).

However, there are laws that God spoke and He still intends for us to obey them today. My family and I believe that when God said in Leviticus 27:30–32 that a tithe of everything we have belongs to Him, that He still means for us to give a tenth of everything to Him even today. This tenth not only includes our money, but it also includes our talents, gifts, time, and all of our belongings. God said to have no other gods before Him and I believe He still today intends for me to put Him first in my life above everything else.

Christians debate rules and laws and whether they were meant for us today, or they were meant for Old Testament living only. Do not get caught up in this argument. Write down what Paul says in 2 Timothy 2:23–24. _____

_____

_____ His answer to the above debate is found in Galatians 2:21. What does he say? _____

_____

_____

Jesus Himself got tested with the same debate in Matthew 22:34–40. He gave only two rules. Write them here:

    1. _____

    2. _____

Write Matthew 22:40 _____

_____

If I love Jesus Christ with all my heart, soul, and mind then I will want to please Him and live righteous according to His word. I want to pay a tithe of all of my income, time, and possessions to help His kingdom. It is very simple: love Him above all things, and love everyone else more than you love yourself. Pray and ask God to place His law in your mouth and not let it depart. Meditate on this day and night. _____

_____

_____

_____

_____

_____

_____

_____

# If and Then
## Day Five

As we end this time together, I hope that you are a little bit wiser and know the heart of God a little better today than you did eight weeks ago. I pray that you have a new passion to embrace your destiny and a newfound courage to tackle it with God's help.

But before we go our separate ways, I want to spend one last day teaching you a lesson for a lifetime. I hope to sum up the entire week in just a few verses and give an easy way to stay focused on God's law.

Look at Deuteronomy 10:12–13 and copy it below. _____

_____

_____

_____

_____

God is asking you to do five things. Write them below:

1. _____ (v. 12)
2. _____ (v. 12)
3. _____ (v. 12)
4. _____ (v. 12)
5. _____ (v. 13)

In these verses, He asks of us to *fear* the Lord, *walk* in all His ways, *love* Him, *serve* Him by serving others, and *obey* His commands. It is that easy. This is the instruction that you want to write down and meditate on day and night. These five instructions will help you reach the life that God intended for you to have.

The first time I read this passage, I knew it was something that I wanted to remember. As I began to memorize the verse, I discovered a simple acronym: FLOWS.

**F**ear the Lord your God.

**L**ove God.

**O**bserve His commands.

**W**alk in His ways.

**S**erve God by serving others.

His blessing *flows* to those who learn this formula. Fear God with reverence and respect. Recognize that you live and breathe because He allows it and that you are nothing without His permission. Love God with everything in you. Love Him so much that you want nothing more than to be with Him and to serve Him. Obey all of His commandments. Walk in His ways and not in the ways of the world. Be set apart and testify about His ways. And finally, show God your love for Him by serving others. Jesus washed the feet of His friends, fed strangers, and touched the hurting. He did all of these things before He ate. His ministry came first in His life. The answer to finding the key to living life to the fullest lies in the simple word FLOWS.

Look at the last few words in this Scripture (Deuteronomy 10:13). What do you think is meant by "for your own good"? _____ _____ Every command of God is for our own good. God desires for us to live an abundant life. His plan is for you to be prosperous, successful, and full of joy and peace. He gave all of His commands "for your own good." What reason would you have to ignore God's commands, especially when you know that He has given them "for your own good"? Take time now to thank Him for this journey. Reflect on the areas where you have grown and ask Him to reveal places where you still fall short._____

_____

_____

_____

_____

_____

_____

I am so proud of you for hanging in there with me for the last eight weeks. You are the Joshua generation, the generation that will inherit your promises. You have a call to lead. Many are waiting. They are looking for one to stand up for them, one that will rescue them from the bondage of slavery to this world. They are searching for one to reestablish the convictions that have been lost for so long. Stand before them and redraw the line in the sand and lead them with character and in truth. You can be what He created you to be. His grace is sufficient. "Consecrate yourselves, for tomorrow the Lord will do amazing things among you" (Joshua 3:5).

Father God, Your word that goes out from Your mouth will not return to You void, but it will accomplish what You desire and achieve the purpose for which You sent it. I pray that these words from You will fall on the fertile soil of the precious hearts that read them and they will begin to bring forth fruit according to Your purpose. Preserve the purpose of each young person who is seeking to know Your heart now. Holy Spirit, give them wisdom when the answer is unclear, show them direction when they are lost, provide courage in the face of adversity, and strength when their bodies and minds grow weary. Help them keep their eyes on You only.

In the name of Your son, Jesus,

Amen.

# Discussion Questions

The following questions are not meant to be used as a substitute for your involvement and discussion with your small group. They are simply a jumping off point in case you get stuck. There is nothing that can replace your guidance and direction. You know your students and what they may need. Be vulnerable and use your own life lessons as examples to instruct them on not only what to do but also what *not* to do.

I would love to hear from you and how this study has impacted your group. Tell us about the growth and struggles that they are experiencing. Contact us on our website, www.myjoshuaproject.com, with questions, concerns, and stories about how God is raising up leaders who once were dormant. "Today I will begin to exalt you in the eyes of all Israel, so they may know that I am with you as I was with Moses" (Joshua 3:7).

## Pre-study introduction

1. In your own words, what is the definition of leadership?

2. Name a few leaders who come to mind (old, young, historical, biblical, male, female, dead, or alive).

3. What made them different from others? Why were they able to lead?

4. In life, you are either leading or following. Can you do both? What about at the same time? Give an example of how that might work.

5. Why do you think people choose to lead?

## Week One

1. God's desire for every born-again Christian is to be what, or to lead others where?

2. To lead others to righteousness you first have to become righteous. What does it mean to be "righteous"?

3. How does it feel to find out that God took the time to hand-make you?

4. What does "influence" mean to you?

5. Who have you influenced this week?

6. Have you recognized this week that you have been guilty of a negative influence?

## Week Two

1. Did this week's study help you recognize that you were in leadership training?

2. Have you been leading where He has placed you as you learn?

3. How can you know God's ways?

4. Which habits do you need to create to mold you into a better leader?

5. What is keeping you from doing these things now?

## Week Three

1. Why is it important for you to become a servant in God's kingdom?

2. Why does God test his children?

3. Can you think of a time in your life where you didn't understand God's way but submitted fully to Him anyway?

4. What was the outcome?

5. Can you remember a time when you disobeyed God's voice and what the consequences of that disobedience were?

# Week Four

1. What are some disciplines where you struggle that are relative to this week's study that was not discussed in the text?

2. Did you discover some new areas in your life where you need to practice self-discipline?

3. Can you think of a person that you feel models self-control?

4. What is the hardest behavior in your life to conquer and model discipline?

5. Is your self-discipline noticeable enough for you to be set apart?

# Week Five

1. What are some things that you are afraid of when thinking about leading your friends and family to lives of righteousness?

2. Can you remember a time when fear changed your perspective about a situation?

3. Fear shows a lack of trust in God. Do you worry too much about particular situations? Why is it so hard for you to relinquish all things to God?

4. Do you have a better understanding of the fear of God? Do you still have unanswered questions?

5. What can you do to begin to walk in the fear of God?

# Week Six

1. How do others describe your reputation?

2. What is your character? Does it demonstrate the character of God?

3. Can you give an example of a test that helped build your character?

4. What does your fruit say about your character?

5. Do you have areas in your life where you need to crucify your flesh and sinful desires?

## Week Seven

1.  Does your character allow you to be trusted? Do others have confidence in you?

2.  Are your thoughts fixed solely on Jesus? Have you entertained impure thoughts?

3.  How do you handle your mistakes? Do you accept responsibility or do you pass blame or deny them?

4.  Can you think of an example where someone has intentionally deceived others to benefit himself or herself?

5.  Do you have a pride issue making it difficult to accept when you are wrong?

6.  Have you violated the trust with those around you that you lead?

## Week Eight

1.  Give an example of an unconditional promise.

2.  Give an example of a conditional promise of God.

3.  What are God's promises for those who obey His commandments? What is the consequence for those who do not obey?

4.  Explain Matthew 22:40 and how the two laws Jesus gave in Matthew 22:34–39 work in conjunction with each other.

5.  Explain and then memorize the acronym FLOWS.

# Endnotes

[1] John C. Maxwell, *Developing the Leader Within You* (Nashville, TN: Thomas Nelson, 1993), 1.

[2] John C. Maxwell, *21 Irrefutable Laws of Leadership: Follow Them and People Will Follow You* (Nashville, TN: Thomas Nelson, 1998 and 2007), 23.

[3] John C. Maxwell, *The 21 Indispensable Qualities of a Leader* (Nashville, TN: Thomas Nelson, 1999), 125.

[4] "Discipline." *The New International Webster's Pocket Dictionary of the English Language* (New Revised ed., 1997).

[5] Francis Chan, *Crazy Love: Overwhelmed by a Relentless God* ( Colorado Springs, CO: David C. Cook, 2008),

[6] "Character." *Dictionary.com Unabridged* (Random House, Inc. August 30, 2010) http://dictionary.reference.com/browse/character>.

[7] "Fornication." *The New International Webster's Pocket Dictionary of the English Language* (New Revised ed., 1997).

[8] John C. Maxwell, *21 Irrefutable Laws of Leadership: Follow Them and People Will Follow You* (Nashville, TN: Thomas Nelson, 1998 and 2007), 64.

[9] Craig Weatherup, as quoted in John C. Maxwell, *21 Irrefutable Laws of Leadership: Follow Them and People Will Follow You* (Nashville, TN: Thomas Nelson, 1998 and 2007), 64.

Printed in the United States
By Bookmasters